MOVIE PALACES

15—

D1520123

BY JOSEPH M. VALERIO
University of Wisconsin–Milwaukee

AND DANIEL FRIEDMAN

EDITED BY
NANCY MORISON AMBLER

MOVIE PALACES
RENAISSANCE AND REUSE

EDUCATIONAL FACILITIES LABORATORIES DIVISION

ACADEMY FOR EDUCATIONAL DEVELOPMENT / PUBLISHERS

MOVIE PALACES: RENAISSANCE AND REUSE was made possible by a grant from the National Endowment for the Arts Design Arts Program.

FRONT COVER: Proscenium arch and sidewalls of the Tampa Theatre, Tampa, Florida. The Spanish Revival house, designed by John Eberson and constructed in 1926, was restored and reopened in 1977 as the central focus of an office/theater/ retail complex.

TITLE PAGE: Powell Symphony Hall in St. Louis on Opening Night, 1968. Designed by Rapp and Rapp, the French baroque St. Louis Theatre built in 1926 is now the home of the St. Louis Symphony Orchestra. The former movie palace is widely recognized as one of the most acoustically superior concert halls in the United States.

This book was designed by Betty Binns, Betty Binns Graphics, New York. The typeface is Gill Sans Light, designed by Eric Gill in 1928. Type was set by U. S. Lithograph, Inc., New York. The printer was Mercantile Printing Company, Worcester, Massachusetts.

ISBN 0 88481 248 0

First published in 1982 by Educational Facilities Laboratories Division, Academy for Educational Development, 680 Fifth Avenue, New York, New York 10019
© Educational Facilities Laboratories 1982

CONTENTS

ACKNOWLEDGEMENTS

Movie Palaces: Renaissance and Reuse represents a cooperative venture funded by the National Endowment for the Arts, Design Arts Program, in which Educational Facilities Laboratories served as editor and publisher, and Joseph Valerio and Daniel Friedman as authors. The offices of both EFL in New York and Chrysalis Corp. Architects in Milwaukee were used for project administration, research, and production purposes.

Both EFL and the School of Architecture and Urban Planning at the University of Wisconsin-Milwaukee, where Mr. Valerio is a professor, have been active for a number of years in the historic preservation and adaptive reuse of older structures. EFL, a nonprofit organization established in 1958 to guide and encourage constructive change in education and other "people-serving" institutions, was among the first organizations to advocate adaptive reuse as an historic preservation option. In 1974, EFL published *Reusing Railroad Stations*, a seminal work in the field of historic preservation and adaptive reuse, followed the next year by *Reusing Railroad Stations, Book Two*. In 1976, EFL published *The Arts in Found Places*, a documentation of arts activities housed in buildings originally created for another purpose. The three works (each supported with funding from the National Endowment for the Arts) helped local governments, citizen groups, and developers across the country to reuse abandoned stations for combined public and commercial purposes, including arts and educational centers, transportation hubs, and focal points for municipal redevelopment.

In 1978, EFL President Alan C. Green proposed to the Endowment a book on the reuse of movie palaces. In the same year, Malcolm Holzman, FAIA, Principal, Hardy Holzman Pfeiffer Associates, New York, conducted a Graduate Research Studio, "Movie Palaces of the 1920s and 1930s," at the University of Wisconsin-Milwaukee. The Studio was funded by a grant from the Eschweiler Foundation, Milwaukee, and participants presented the results of their research at a day-long seminar held at the University.

Based on the success of and information gleaned during the Eschweiler Studio, Dean Anthony J. Catanese of the University of Wisconsin-Milwaukee School of Architecture and Urban Planning and Mr. Valerio conceived the idea of a three-day national symposium, "The American Movie Palace." The symposium was held in Milwaukee in April 1980 under the aegis of the School of Architecture and Urban Planning, and Mr. Valerio subsequently proposed to the Endowment a book highlighting the papers presented at the symposium.

Recognizing that, working together, EFL and Mr. Valerio could produce a valuable publication, Michael J. Pittas, Director of the National Endowment for the Arts Design Arts Program, encouraged and arranged the joint venture. Lance Brown and Fifi Sheridan of the Design Arts Program worked closely with the parties to achieve the necessary coordination. Mr. Valerio then engaged Mr. Friedman, co-director of the symposium and a graduate of the School of Architecture, as coauthor.

Nancy Morison Ambler, an EFL project director with a special interest in preservation and conservation issues, was asked to edit and produce the book. (In her former position as public relations coordinator for the Opera Company of Boston, Miss Ambler spent many hours watching company productions at Boston's Orpheum Theatre, a 1920s vaudeville house.) EFL's Beryl Fields, Rhoda Kraus, and Elizabeth Gay word processed the manuscript which was copy edited by Charlotte Gross. The book was designed by Betty Binns, who for many years has been art director of *Theater Crafts* magazine.

With grateful appreciation, we wish to thank the following individuals and organizations for helping to make possible the research and publication of *Movie Palaces: Renaissance and Reuse*.

Douglas Gomery, Professor of Communication Arts at the University of Maryland, was a great help throughout the period of research, writing, and editing, sharing insights and valuable information from his own archives.

Hugh Hardy, FAIA, Principal, Hardy Holzman Pfeiffer Associates, New York, under a Design Project Fellowship from the National Endowment for the Arts, established avenues of communication with a number of individuals who helped to provide information on movie palaces.

The contribution of the late Gene Chesley, a founder of the League of Historic American Theatres and compiler of the National List of Historic Theatre Buildings, must not go unrecognized. His life's work was devoted to the preservation of American movie theaters.

For reading and critiquing the manuscript, along with Malcolm Holzman, Douglas Gomery, and Joseph Duci Bella, Chicago area director of the Theatre Historical Society, we wish to thank Rosemarie Bletter, Assistant Professor of Architectural History at Columbia University. Miss Bletter, coauthor of *Skyscraper Style*, offered a number of points about the architectural history of the movie palace era.

Susan Tunick, an artist in New York, was generous in providing information and photographic documentation on terra-cotta.

Eschweiler Studio participants whose research is included in this book are: Michael Borski, Cyrus Fishburn, Patrick Fitzgerald, Philip Hamp, Andrea Landsman, Robert Storm, and Diane Turner.

Together with Mr. Valerio, Vince James of Chrysalis Corp. Architects, and Paul Mueller and Michael Hayes, architecture students at the University of Wisconsin-Milwaukee, produced a number of theater site plan and section drawings included in this publication.

For their generous assistance in helping us to compile case study information, we thank: Mrs. Mary Bishop, Director of Building Development and Grants, Columbus Association for the Performing Arts; Richard F. McCann, AIA, Principal, R.F. McCann & Company, Seattle; Roger A. Phillips, AIA, Principal, Arendt/Mosher/Grant/Pedersen/Phillips, Santa Barbara; Michael Newman, FAIA, Principal, Newman Calloway Johnson Winfree, Winston-Salem; Nananne Porcher, Principal, Jean Rosenthal Associates, Orange, New Jersey; Samuel M. Stone, Director of Development, North Carolina School of the Arts, Winston-Salem; Charles Raison, Executive Director, and Jane Kirkham, Director of Planning and Development, Playhouse Square Foundation, Cleveland; Gregory L. Gilmore, Executive Director, and Dulcie C. Gilmore, Director of Marketing, Aurora Civic Center Authority/Aurora Redevelopment Commission; Harvey Hoshour, AIA, Albuquerque; Robert Cannon, Executive Director, Arts Council of San Antonio; Leon Gennette, President, Brown Grand Opera House, Inc., Concordia, Kansas; P.T. Michaels & Associates, New York.

We also acknowledge with gratitude the assistance of the hundreds of additional community leaders, administrators, theater management personnel, designers, historians, arts advocates, and technicians who have shared with us their myriad experiences and knowledge in the sphere of theater arts, operations, and adaptive use. Without their patient and detailed explanations of how their own programs are organized and managed, we would have been unable to produce this study.

FOREWORD

The Orpheum, the Savoy, the Imperial, the Majestic—the movie palace names march by summoning heady images of Indo-European splendor and Art Deco elegance, of stage and screen stars, of gala opening nights sparkling with shiny limousines, silk top hats, and the pulsating lights of photographers' flashbulbs.

Sentimental images aside—but with dreams still very much in focus—movie palaces remain as important today as they were to Hollywood's Golden Age. Prior to 1900, not a single structure had been built specifically for use as a movie theater. Less than 30 years later, however, movie palaces great and small could be found across the United States. Every major crossroads had its own Roxy or Grand—"an acre of seats in a garden of dreams"—to which the wealthy and not-so-wealthy could escape into a luxurious setting that swept them away from their own time and place.

From 1915-1945, over 4,000 movie palaces (and thousands more smaller theaters) were constructed, several hundred films were released, and audiences that numbered in the hundreds of thousands applauded those films and the stage extravaganzas that often preceded and followed them. The palaces themselves figured prominently in the rise of Hollywood's Golden Age and its accompanying glamour, and, as *Movie Palaces: Renaissance and Reuse* discusses, in the universal appeal of film and the democratization of the cinema arts.

Despite their imperiled position (on one side of the tightrope lies destruction, on the other, revitalization) movie palaces are as important now as in that long past Golden Age, and for a number of reasons. First, they are important as a unique building type of the 20th century—the fusion of architectural design, economics, entertainment, and technology. Although architectural historians have only recently begun to take the palaces seriously, the structures' calculated bravura belies their technological advances and pragmatically-inspired imaginative design. The original palace architects and the palaces themselves rose to the task demanded of them by the movie moguls and, in time, the cinema patrons: to provide a larger-than-life showcase for a larger-than-life medium. Furthermore, their attention to detail and ingenious treatment of space demand more than superficial attention from architects, architectural historians, and the general public. The palaces and their smaller neighborhood contemporaries proffered a fitting setting for the screen giants—and their devoted fans—to play out their roles.

Second, in addition to their importance as a building type, movie palaces provide a concrete link with our past. The Bijou and the Oriental represent a segment of America's Main Street. To see a unit etched in our cultural memory reduced to rubble is a disturbing experience, one that severs tangible connections to our individual and collective heritage. America's historic preservation movement has come of age in the past 15 years, but the occasional crunch of the wrecker's ball as it connects with that past—the subsequent crumble of favorite minarets, gilt staircases, halls of mirrors, and polychromed murals—reminds us that preservation advocacy for the potential renaissance of movie palaces and other older buildings ought to be accelerated, not relaxed.

Movie palaces have the potential to be more than a museum for an interested or curious few, an albatross awaiting demolition. On the contrary, they can function—and have demonstrated as much in many such projects across the country—as glorious spaces for the performing arts and other users, as a magnet to help attract an estranged public back into city life during the hours when most downtown workplaces have been abandoned for suburban homes. In Cleveland, Aurora, Winston-Salem, San Antonio, and many other cities, aging theaters have become the centerpiece for major downtown redevelopment efforts. In Seattle, Atlanta, Columbus, St. Louis and countless other locales, reprogrammed movie palaces have served to stimulate the commercial vitality and cultural substance of the central business district.

The renaissance of the movie palace, then, represents more than the preservation of an important building type and a link with the past. Economically, restoration has proved more cost-effective in relationship to yield than new construction. Furthermore, if education, energy conservation, accessibility of the arts, creation of new jobs, and renewed urban vitality are added to the basic dividends, the actual value of each relit movie palace marquee surely exceeds quantifiable statistics.

The renaissance of America's movie palaces and neighborhood theaters is of especial interest to us at the Design Arts Program of the National Endowment for the Arts. Their revitalization and reuse represents themes which stimulate our ongoing interest and support.

□   Design, as an art form, merits public and critical attention comparable to that paid such arts as opera, sculpture, and the dance.

□   Movie palaces, originally constructed to provide settings for live quality entertainment and the art of the cinema, once again are providing space for the performing arts.

□   Movie palaces, like many other older structures, represent an existing national asset. Their value—commercially and as urban amenities—is no longer a matter of speculation.

□   As concerned citizens and developers participate in the renaissance of movie palaces and other friendly Main Street properties, they and other community members will in turn reap the benefits of such projects: renewed vigor in town, new jobs created by possible movie theater renovation construction and citizens returning to downtown, and the positive community spirit fostered by those cultural assets which help make a city "livable."

We are pleased to present to you, then, the work of Joseph Valerio and Daniel Friedman, and of Alan Green and Nancy Ambler at Educational Facilities Laboratories, what we believe to be a well researched, judiciously edited, and beautifully produced publication. As we introduce this book, we believe that it will serve many people and many purposes. We anticipate that it will increase awareness on the part of architects, engineers, theater designers, planners, community organizations, individuals at all levels of government, and private developers of the potential advantages of adapting movie palaces as cultural and other public-serving facilities, and as catalysts for downtown renewal. The grand-scale palaces as well as the smaller neighborhood houses have new roles to play in the life of cities and their individual communities.

It is our expectation that an awareness of such reuse potential will stimulate local planners, developers, and arts and community groups to consider the adaptive potential of other older structures—factories, railroad stations, mills, and schools, for instance. Finally, we hope that you will find *Movie Palaces: Renaissance and Reuse* helpful as you contribute to the relighting of theater marquees in your own towns and cities, and in so doing become a part of the community spirit and pride that come with opening night and each night thereafter.

Michael J. Pittas
Director, Design Arts Program
National Endowment for the Arts

INTRODUCTION

Movie Palaces: Renaissance and Reuse explores the potential of America's movie theaters—great and small—as an important national asset. Each of the 4,000 palaces constructed during Hollywood's Golden Age, as well as the countless smaller theaters built during that era and modeled after the grander showcases, has a role to play in the life of our cities and towns today.

The American movie palace and its smaller relative—the neighborhood movie house—differ more in size and seating capacity than in decor and the ability to support live performance. Most theater historians agree that although no real formula distinguishes the palace from the smaller house, movie palaces share certain characteristics.

☐ Most movie palaces seat between 1,000 and 5,000 patrons. Other movie houses seat fewer than 1,000 persons.

☐ Movie palaces have a stage and stagehouse with fly loft, rigging, dressing rooms, and orchestra pit. Many smaller theaters lack full stagehouse and orchestra facilities.

☐ Movie palaces have a balcony, often supplemented with a mezzanine and additional seating levels. Many smaller houses were constructed without balconies.

☐ Movie palaces and many smaller houses have a noticeable (if not dominant) decorative personality. Smaller houses, however, cannot claim the rich ornamentation found in the palaces.

☐ Movie palaces were, by definition, designed to launch and promote new films. Smaller theaters generally were second- and third-run outlets. Because the reputation of films was established in the downtown showcases, smaller theaters, capitalizing on opening promotional campaigns and favorable first reviews, did not require the palaces' elaborate settings and grand-scale entertainment to attract moviegoers.

☐ Movie palaces were constructed in the downtown areas of cities, and typically clustered in existing entertainment districts on turf already well established by vaudeville. Boston, Chicago, Cleveland, Minneapolis, New York, and Philadelphia are among those cities which contain multiblock clusters of theaters. Smaller theaters dotted the secondary commercial districts of outlying urban neighborhoods, small cities, and rural towns. By 1930, the smaller houses outnumbered movie palaces nearly seven to one.

☐ Movie palaces appear in several development contexts, each of which can play a significant role in a theater's adaptive potential. The palaces were first constructed as freestanding theaters, or as theaters sharing a wall with adjacent but otherwise unrelated commercial structures. Later, between 1925 and 1930, they were designed as a component—usually the central core—of larger, multistoried office buildings.

Large first-run movie palaces are also found on major commercial thoroughfares and at intersections served by principal transportation routes. These outlying middle-city districts were generally supported by several contiguous residential neighborhoods. Strips of theaters were often built as the featured element of two- and three-story multi-use retail complexes. Small storefront shops generally flanked the theater entrances, unified by the theaters' decorative theme. Offices or apartments were often located on the upper floors of the complex. The size and seating capacity of outlying first-run theaters reflect the velocity of competition among rival exhibitors. As a rule, the greater the distance from either the central business district or its primary commercial satellites, the smaller the theater.

Architectural elements of a movie palace. Legend: 1, marquee; 2, outer lobby; 3, inner lobbies; 4, mechanical systems (heating, ventilating, and lighting equipment and panels); 5, mixed use (rental offices, apartments, commercial space); 6, theater administrative offices; 7, artists warm-up, costume and scene shops; 8, orchestra seating; 9, balcony seating; 10, sound reflector; 11, orchestra pit; 12, stage; 13, rigging and fly loft; 14, proscenium arch.

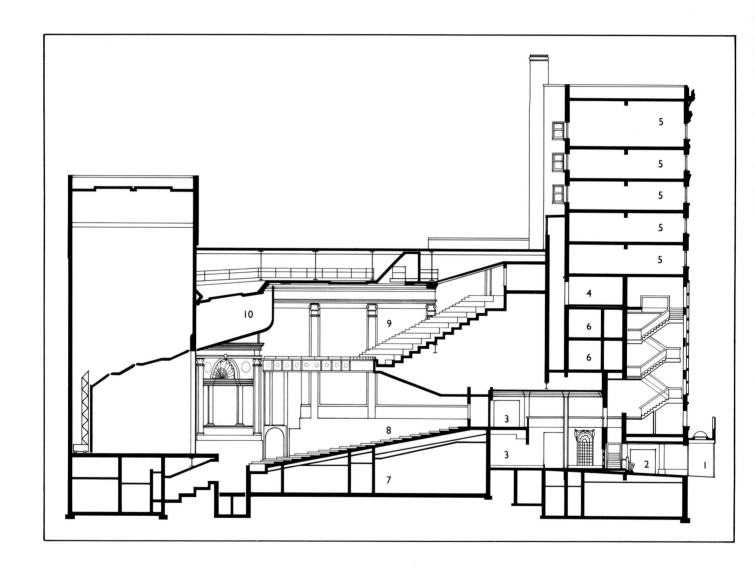

The diagram on the preceding page details a typical movie palace and its architectural parts—the auditorium, proscenium, fly loft, balconies, lobby, and other areas mentioned throughout this report. All or some of these theater parts can be altered or left basically untouched in the renaissance of a house.

Herein lies a confusing stereotype. Terms such as "renaissance," "restoration," and "reprogramming" often conjure images of extensive interior and exterior demolition and ensuing construction. In some cases, the renaissance of a movie theater need involve only surface reappointments such as careful cleaning and painting, and replacing spent light bulbs. In other cases, theater projects will involve such major renovation work as changing the seating capacity of the hall, enlarging the stage and wings area, and constructing additional theaters within the original space. Generally, most projects involve work that lies somewhere in between these extremes.

Another common misconception about the reuse of movie palaces and other smaller theaters is the very term "reuse." In some cases, use of the theater will go unchanged—movies will continue to be shown. In other cases, films might be shown to earn extra income during periods when live performing arts events are not booked into the house. In still other cases, movies might not be shown at all, with the house adapted for reuse as a symphony hall, retail mall, church, restaurant, or vocational education facility. The most common "reuse" of a movie palace, however, is as a performing arts facility, a use to which the palaces—with their balconies, stages, rigging, and fly lofts—lend themselves well.

Movie Palaces is divided into three major sections. The first explores the social and economic history of the movie palace—the significance of the phenomenon. The second consists of case studies, drawn from projects nationwide, which reflect the programming options for theater renaissance. The third section, which profiles the lessons of the second, includes planning guidelines for theater economic feasibility studies, organizational structures, program environments, and adaptive reuse and operating costs. Finally, a resource list of publications and organizations offers encouragement to readers as they relight movie palace marquees in their own communities.

THE PAST OF
THE FUTURE

THE MOVIE PALACE PHENOMENON

Although the movie palace was the product of powerful and unprecedented forces synthesized at the turn of the century, it belongs to a family of buildings that reaches across 2,400 years of Western history. Theater and the structure in which it is housed are vital expressions of culture that have evolved to suit the ongoing public demand for drama, spectacle, and entertainment. As a showcase for spectacle, the movie palace is the 20th-century continuum of theater history.

The first palatial movie theater was constructed in Paris in 1910. Originally built as a legitimate theater called the Hippodrome, it was converted to the 5,000-seat Gaumont-Palace which featured rear-projected cinema. (1) Three years later, Thomas Lamb's Regent Theatre in New York City became the first movie palace built in the United States. As one opening night reviewer wrote: "[The Regent has] an environment so pleasing, so perfect in artistic detail, that it seems as if the setting were a prerequisite to the picture, that to an educated audience the two should, and must hereafter, go together." (2)

Although the size and decor of its successors would render it a modest theater by comparison, the lighting of the Regent's marquee signaled the beginning of Hollywood's Golden Age—the three decades when film production and audiences reached their numerical zenith. The first 20 years of that golden age saw the construction of nearly 4,000 movie palaces designed to accommodate both live, stage-born theatrical entertainment and the relatively new two-dimensional medium of film.

The movie palace began as an embellished version of a vaudeville theater, modified over time to support the exhibition of silent moving pictures. Hollywood's corporate leaders recognized the potential of such hybrid packaging to win larger audiences and promote a new hybrid product. Attendance figures climbed on company charts, yielding both profit and the unexpected social consequence of shrewd marketing: Hollywood had captured the modern American plurality. Opulence had been used for centuries to indicate social rank, but never before the movie palace had it been used to bring together such diverse classes and ethnicities.

Finally, the movie palace expresses 20th-century technology packaged in historic images. The building type emerged during an unusual period, precisely at the edge of revolutionary changes in science, industry, and art. The ingredients of a new epoch—the Bauhaus, Einstein, Joyce, Picasso, Nietzsche, Freud, mass production, radio, automobiles, unions, airplanes, and the far-reaching impact of World War I—were jamming at history's turnstile. The movie palace reflects the intoxicating

(*Preceding page*) This elegant stairway in Rapp and Rapp's 1925 Uptown Theatre in Chicago exemplifies the Beaux Arts tradition in movie palace architecture.

The Alcazar Theatre, a Chicago nickelodeon.

climate of change manifested in the urban excitement of the 1920s. Both as a source of information and as a revolutionary form of entertainment, the movie palace and its unique offering helped to usher in the age.

FILM

It is difficult to disconnect the movie palace as an architectural phenomenon from the equally remarkable development of moving pictures. The history of cinema is, in fact, the most recent development in the history of the performing arts, theater, and theater design.

The first successful attempts to animate photography began, with little regard for the dramatic arts, in the last quarter of the 19th century. The true midwives of Hollywood were neither artists nor playwrights, but scientists, inventors, technicians, and entrepreneurs. Large-screen motion pictures were introduced to the United States in 1896 before the audience of a New York vaudeville house. (3) As a novel filler for a bill of live entertainment, silent pictures posed no great threat to the world of stage. The better vaudeville theaters catered to a middle class sensibility not readily enticed by the somewhat

primitive state of motion picture technology. Film would have to mature elsewhere in the urban population.

According to Robert Sklar, author of *Movie Made America*, "the motion pictures came to life in the United States when they made contact with working class needs and desires." (4) In its early years—1900–1910—film was inexpensive entertainment. However, while working class patronage helped produce the enormous profits that allowed pioneers like Thomas A. Edison to increase productivity while improving the product, the early audiences of the new medium were by no means *limited* to immigrant patronage.

Little more than an indoor space and a screen were all that was needed to satisfy the early film patron who paid admission to see rather than to be seen. The nickelodeon (a term coined by two Pittsburgh entrepreneurs in 1905), the first showcase exclusively for the exhibition of film, was itself basically a room and a screen. By 1909, 8,000 nickelodeons were operating in the United States, over 600 in New York alone. (5) Inexpensive film entertainment made a few enterprising businessmen very wealthy by the end of the first decade of the 20th century.

The stereotypical nickelodeon was a fairly short-lived phenomenon often cited by historians as the exclusive recreation of working class consumers. However, a reevaluation of the early years of movie marketing shows that fierce competition, the limited supply of films, and an early effort to broaden the

Thomas Lamb's 1913 Regent Theatre in New York.

market were ideas that shaped the exhibition business long before the meteoric rise of the major film corporations. (6)

In his analysis of nickelodeons and the New York entertainment districts, historian Robert C. Allen concludes that "as early as 1907....entrepreneurs saw that huge profits could be made by converting large capacity theaters into movie houses, where audiences enjoyed not only movies but the trappings of theatrical entertainment." (7) Clearly, the ingredients of the movie palace experience were being tested well before Samuel I. Rothafel ("Roxy") and his contemporaries took the idea to heroic extremes. Even in the trade press of 1909, as Allen notes, at least one journal anticipated the eclipse of the bare-bones storefront movie houses, "their place being taken by especially built theaters, seating 500 to 1,000, most of them giving a mixed bill of vaudeville and motion pictures." (8)

By 1912, "small-time vaudeville"—a combination of film features and live presentation—had attracted a diverse patronage. Competing with the legitimate houses and nickelodeons of urban entertainment districts, the small-time vaudeville format set the stage for the critical transition that produced Thomas Lamb's 1913 Regent, and several thousand other million-dollar movie palaces. The subsequent synthesis of more sophisticated film productions, mixed billing strategies, and the construction of monumental theaters that connected the new experience of the cinema and the respected architecture of the legitimate stage characterize "the movie palace era."

MARKETING

The early popularity and commercial success of movies in the neighborhoods and entertainment districts of American cities intensified the continuing struggle between rival film companies to control the production, distribution, and exhibition of motion pictures. Thomas Alva Edison was the first overlord of American motion pictures, although his actual contribution to film technology was relatively insignificant. Exercising legal and economic coercion, Edison marshalled nearly all of the existing equipment patents together under a single corporation and in 1908 established the Motion Pictures Patent Company. Known as "the Trust," Edison's organization controlled production and distribution until the growing resistance of independents and a Federal anti-trust suit functionally toppled the monopoly in 1912. The Trust was dismantled by court action in 1917.

Carl Laemmle, a Midwest distributor who broke with the Trust in 1909, was Edison's chief rival. Having adapted the star billing concept from legitimate theater and vaudeville, Laemmle's Chicago-based operation and other strong, independent producers began to reap greater profits from expanding nickelodeon sales. The "star" concept also worked to lure a fresh generation of aspiring performers and technicians from the

The monumental terra-cotta facade of Chicago's 1926 Granada Theatre—a Levy and Klein design—under construction (right).

New York's 1914 Strand Theatre (left), which "started a new style in motion picture theaters."

world of the stage into the business of movie-making, and industry profits and the quality of film steadily improved.

Laemmle helped to soften the market for other independent entrepreneurs such as William Fox and Adolph Zukor. Fox and Zukor (the latter an early affiliate of the Lowe's vaudeville empire) turned their attention to audience expansion. Fox captured the middle class market by exhibiting films in better vaudeville theaters, while Zukor experimented with the format and content of movies. In 1912, he tested his belief that educated audiences would pay to see respectable drama on film. Zukor leased the Lyceum Theatre in New York for a special showing of the full-length French import, *Queen Elizabeth*, starring Sarah Bernhardt in her first movie role. He charged one dollar for admission, a substantial leap—not only in price but psychology—from the nickels of 1909. The exclusive film engagement tapped an audience previously uninterested in silent film entertainment.

D. W. Griffith was as influential behind the camera as Zukor, Fox and Marcus Loew were behind the desk. Griffith's 1913 *Birth of a Nation*, one of the most popular films in history, rewrote the fundamental criteria for film-making, even though it outraged intellectuals with its overt political bias and racial stereotypes. (9) The controversy over Griffith's first masterpiece, however, did not diminish the contribution of his feature-length epic films which accomplished exactly what Zukor had hoped *Queen Elizabeth* would do: they made film respectable middle-class entertainment.

The influence of "movie stars" and feature-length films notwithstanding, entrepreneurs knew that silent moving pictures could not by themselves engender the loyal patronage of a widening urban audience. Seizing the programming concept of the small vaudeville format, Roxy was among the first to perfect the hybrid environment necessary to showcase film successfully. He created for the screen the legitimacy of the real stage, supported by a monumental theater building. Film rode to popularity on the recognized value of live productions and the status associated with architecture of heroic proportions.

Although the Regent was completed first, it was Roxy's management of the Strand that fixed the movie palace formula. When the Strand opened in New York in 1914, it "started a new style in motion picture theaters: comfortable seats, thick rugs, elegant lounges, velvet draperies, gilt-and-marble ornamentation—all the trappings of wealth that had previously belonged to a select few in the orchestra of a legitimate theater—and all for twenty-five cents." (10)

Roxy attacked the problem of promotion with management strategies that focused on the two primary media of moving picture exhibition: the static medium of *place*, and the dynamic medium of *event*. As he said:

Behind the theater there should be an idea, a *living* idea. Behind the programs there should likewise be an animate idea. It is that intangible something, that moving spirit, that makes the theater a *living* factor of local activities and a community center.... (11)

Upper balcony of the 1927 Roxy Theatre, "the largest theater built since the fall of Rome."

The dynamic elements of event included all things animated and changing. The flat grey images of silent moving pictures were enriched by pulsating marquees, white-gloved attendants and ushers in crisp uniforms, perfumed air, changing colored lighting, and the stage production, accompanied by full orchestra, dancers, singers, comics, and actors filling the auditorium with the aura of classic theater. When a large orchestra was inappropriate or too expensive, the theater organist would step in. (12) The elaborate keyboard and pipes of the grand organ were capable of producing the sounds of a variety of musical instruments and ensembles, not to mention special effects. Its crescendo could fill an auditorium with thundering scores or synchopate the denouement of a silent drama. Soon after its introduction in theaters, the organ became a celebrated fixture of picture palace entertainment.

In the Strand and other theaters, these elements of event were experienced in the context of the static architectural setting: the facade; the grand foyer with its baroque staircases and colonnades; the formal lobby; intimate parlors; the paintings, drapery, and wall hangings; the balcony and mezzanine; the enchanted massive auditorium; and, of course, the proscenium arch.

The New York Times compared the opening of the Strand to "a Presidential reception, a first night at the opera." (13) "The finest looking people in town" were suddenly going to the movies in numbers, not so much for the film itself, but for the entertainment extravaganza surrounding it.

Roxy's formula for the first-run movie showcase came to fruition in his magnificent Roxy Theatre. Opened in 1927, the New York showcase featured the most extravagant interior decor he could conjure out of architects and designers. Hollywood historian Kenneth Macgowan elaborates:

The Roxy was to top them all.... with 6,200 (seats). The largest theater built since the fall of Rome had six box offices, room for 2,000 people to wait .... while beguiled by an automatic organ, a hospital with two nurses, and.... a huge radio station....
Backstage, 150 people danced, sang, ran lights, or shifted scenery. Another 150 were busy in the front of the house, four-fifths of them ushers. (14)

Roxy trafficked in splendor. Nothing was overlooked, nothing left unembellished.

Nearly all of the 4,000 first-run and deluxe neighborhood movie palaces subscribed to Roxy's showcase formula designed to tap the drawing power of live performance and film in an opulent environment. The stage house and fly loft—elements of legitimate theater so essential to live performance—became an integral part of the movie palace entertainment package, and it is this marketing decision which is the key reason that movie palaces are today especial candidates for revitalization as cultural facilities.

Multi-colored decorative element on a 1912 Thomas Lamb vaudeville house—later a movie palace, still later the Audubon Ballroom —in New York. The rich colors on the terra-cotta piece include green, blue, yellow, white, mustard, tan, and brown.

ARCHITECTURAL ELEMENTS OF FANTASY

The environment of the movie palace appealed simultaneously to self-esteem and fantasy. Its decoration was far more impressionistic than the interior of its closest antecedent, the 19th-century opera house. The experience of a movie palace —its aural, visual, and even olfactory sensations—insulated patrons from the commonplace. Most importantly, the world of the movie palace invited a suspension of disbelief commensurate with the product its environment was designed to sell. As palace architect Thomas Lamb prescribed:

To make our audience receptive and interested, we must cut them off from the rest of the city life and take them into a rich and self-contained auditorium, where their minds are freed from their usual occupations and freed from their customary thoughts. In order to do this, it is necessary to present to their eyes a general scheme quite different from their daily environment, quite different in color scheme, and a great deal more elaborate. (15)

Each element of the theater, from street to screen, was an extension of stagecraft. The fantasy began with the facade. Its height and strong vertical lines, accentuated by ascending pilasters, windows, and towers, lifted the eye above the traditional shop fronts, signaling to those who would enter its elegant portals an experience far different from that of the every day.

The ornate application of terra-cotta cladding allowed movie palace designers to distinguish the theater facade from those of neighboring buildings. Terra-cotta appeared as an exterior cladding for the first time in the last quarter of the 19th century. Virtually fireproof and impervious to moisture, it became particularly appealing to architects after the great fires in Chicago and San Francisco. The clay could be molded or modeled according to architects' specifications, and the use of glazes allowed manufacturers to develop tones and textures that imitated prohibitively expensive materials such as marble and granite. By the 1920s, terra-cotta was recognized in its own right as a vehicle not only for imitation, but also as a source of exotic color and ornamentation. The brilliant terra-cotta purples, golds, azures, and crimsons are colors that had never before and have not since been achieved as a permanent architectural image.

The marquee, as well, extended the theatrical medium from stage to street. Like the movies themselves, its heroic image was designed to extend the limits of its impact. It was animate, performing for the crowds seeking admission to the theater, and alerting those for blocks around to the excitement that

The gradiose marquee of Chicago's Granada Theatre.

The Spanish baroque grand stair of Chicago's palatial Uptown Theatre.

awaited them at the movies. The pulsating sign also separated the movie palace from its more lofty precedent, the classical theater, thus strengthening the practical connection between production and patron on the street.

Once inside the theater, the patron moved through a series of circulation and waiting areas. The space assigned to the entrance vestibule, foyers, lobbies, lounges, upper level promenades, and waiting rooms were functions of comfort, safety, and promotion. Lobbies became monumental antechambers designed to whet the imagination of a large crowd. Rapp and Rapp senior architect E.C.A. Bullock described their architectural intent in a 1925 *Architectural Forum* article:

.... the lobby must be a place of real interest, a place where the waiting throng may be transformed.... The walls and surfaces of the lobby should.... (permit) the theatergoers to get one vista after another, which will produce.... a desire to gain admittance to other parts of the house. In other words, the lobby should be so designed and so equipped that the fascination resulting from it will keep the mind of the patron off the fact that he is waiting.... (16)

Many designers also treated the grand stair as an element of considerable object-value, recalling baroque prototypes of the 18th century. Massive balustrades, low risers, elliptical treads, red carpets, minimized runs, and generous width were devices frequently used to "give the impression that the upper most seats in the balcony were in no way difficult to reach." (17) The stairway, then, as well as columns, pilasters, and the vertical proportions of lobby space, enticed movement toward the upper levels, acting as "an invitation to ascend." (18)

All ancillary space in the theater anticipated the auditorium. In this enormous room endowed with distant ritual and myth, columns, niches, arches, pediments, ceiling vaulting, statuary, and a vast assembly of other ornamental parts were washed in changing colored light that distorted size and hid imperfection. Most important, the ethereal light helped to establish a critical "other worldliness," that sense of removal from the ordinary environment.

The theatrical mechanics of movie palace special effects are described in program notes prepared for the opening of Chicago's Uptown. Designed by Rapp and Rapp in 1925, the Uptown was the largest theater in the Balaban and Katz chain.

All light on the auditorium ceiling is from coves and hidden grilles, unseen by the eye and controlled by the multi-colored system from the colossal dimmer-board back stage. This dimmer-board permits the mixing of colors to any degree or in any form anywhere in the whole house. Some 17,000 electric light bulbs are used in the theater. (19)

The lights of the auditorium played on surfaces of terracotta, brick, plaster, and scagliola, all designed to heighten the moviegoer's sense of detachment from the every day world. Scagliola, a cousin of cast plaster, was frequently used in the

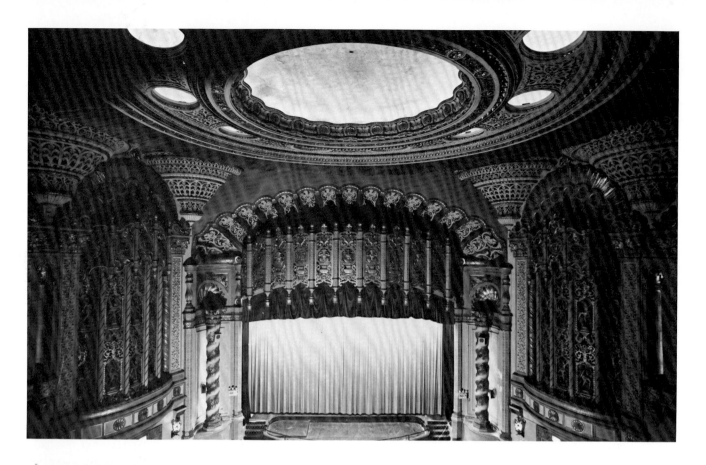

The magnificently ornamented auditorium (above) of Chicago's United Artists Theatre. Detail photograph (left) shows ceiling and sidewall vaulting in the movie palace, a 1928 C. Howard Crane design.

Ornamental plasterwork baroque arches in Chicago's 1926 Palace Theatre, a Rapp and Rapp design.

construction of balustrades, columns, and heavier decorative elements. Over a substratum of glues and ground gypsum, artisans stirred granite dust, pulverized marble, and other additives into the soft surface to create the appearance of variegated ornamental stone. For wall surfaces, plaster catalogues in wide circulation offered thousands of decorative finishes borrowed from the historic design vocabulary.

The movie palace facade, marquee, interior spaces, and lighting were all real or imagined buttresses for the proscenium arch—the focus of the auditorium and the symbol of Roxy's marketing strategy. Developed during the Renaissance, the proscenium is the crucial link between the world of the audience and the world of the performer. It is the window through which spectators gain a different view of their lives and their world. Roxy's successful transference of the proscenium arch from legitimate theater to film showcases proved a common denominator which helped a skeptical audience accept the new medium.

ARCHITECTURAL STYLE

The architects of American movie palaces were influenced by an urban landscape replete with historical allusions. Historian Walter Kidney suggests that the eclectic designer of the late

19th and early 20th centuries, in a profession-wide overturning of Victorian sensibility, "saw himself as a participant in.... a reform movement that had restored taste and literacy to architecture." (20)

Without doubt, the great expositions of the era—the Columbian World at Chicago in 1893, the Louisiana Purchase at St. Louis in 1904, the Panama Pacific at San Francisco in 1915, and the Panama California at San Diego in 1916—provided the theater architect with a useful repository of historical images. In fact, the architectural commission for the exposition in Chicago, a panel top-heavy with East Coast architects, sought consciously to fashion its predominantly neoclassical vocabulary into a national building style. The architects had received their professional training in Paris at the Ecole des Beaux Arts, where neoclassicism was the pedagogical norm. Architect Richard Morris Hunt, speaking for the Commission, asserted that the Corinthian temples constructed for the Exposition should serve as an object lesson to the United States. (21) The temporary buildings of the Exposition "changed the fashion in America from Richardsonian to classic .... a new style in the United States (which) came via the East Coast." (22)

The Beaux Arts aesthetic incorporated rational planning and design based on the proposed function of a building and the historical style selected by the architect to serve as a model for the structure. The architectural "object lesson" in Chicago fostered a uniquely American revival of historical

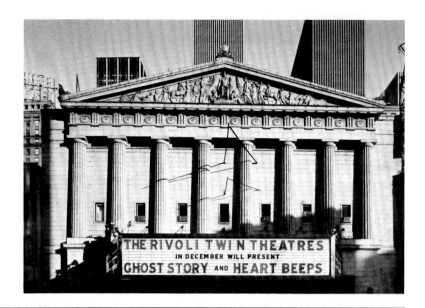

The neoclassical white terra-cotta-clad facade of New York's Rivoli Theatre, a 1917 Thomas Lamb design. The movie palace is slated for restoration and reuse as a legitimate stage.

styles. Other expositions added new styles to the ecletic palette, each addition disseminated to American architectural firms in the pages of trade journals and product bulletins. With the help of catalogues and mass production, American designers took to their boards with a refreshed enthusiasm for ornament, culling the best of the architectural history of Europe. Armed with their sophisticated knowledge of architectural history, the architects creatively combined the best of varied styles to design new and imaginative structures.

Buildings were fashioned after renaissance prototypes from Italy, England, and Holland, and architects experimented with gothic, Jacobean, Lombardic, Greek, and Imperial Roman themes. The academic sensation of Chicago's "white city" was all but overwhelmed by an architectural heterogeneity that served to enrich the popular imagination, invariably enriching the fantasy of movie palaces.

In the early 1920s, the aristocratic pretense of theater decor inspired by European renaissance, baroque, and rococo design was supplemented by the motifs of exotic cultures. Competition among film distributors had replaced the challenge of introducing a new medium as the key marketing issue, and movie palace architects strived to emphasize the thematic diferences between theaters. For instance, Egyptology, fashionable after the 1922 discovery of King Tutankhamen's tomb, inspired several theater entrepreneurs to commission imitations of monumental sanctuaries found near Cairo.

The mid-1920s witnessed the introduction of yet another architectural style, originating like the others in European theory and fashion, but this time altogether discreet from its predecessors. The temperament of the new style—Art Deco—was suggested in official announcements for the *Exposition des Arts Decoratifs et Industriels Modernes*, which launched the style in Paris in 1925. Exposition organizers emphatically prohibited "reproductions, imitations, and counterfeits of ancient styles." (23)

Le Corbusier, one of the great prophets of modern architecture, noted at the time that the Exposition "finally demonstrated the pointlessness of backward glances, [that] a new page was turned." (24) Later, architectural historian Reyner Banham reiterated: "[The Exposition] has its place in the history of western taste....as the source of the popular jazz-modern style." (25)

The character of Art Deco reflects a collision of classical romance and machine-age geometry. Various metallic finishes (particularly aluminum and stainless steel) replaced the traditional use of polished stone and its imitations; statuary and classical minutiae were abandoned in favor of hard lined geometries, chevrons, zigzags, and stylized floral motifs; instead of heavily encrusted, highly modeled surfaces, Deco walls were rendered in intricate, angular patterns, waving curves, and low relief.

Streamline Moderne appeared later, after 1930, as a further purification of Deco. Moderne buildings are characterized by flat roofs, smooth wall finishes (especially stucco), cylindrical corners, and a "wind tunnel" profile suggesting the speed of locomotives, airplanes, and ocean liners. Both Deco and

A fanciful plaster griffon in Chicago's Palace
Theatre auditorium.

Crimson light plays upward from stylized Art
Deco column capitals, illuminating the Paramount
Arts Centre in Aurora, Illinois.

Streamline Moderne auditorium of Philadelphia's 1938 Chelten Theatre.

Moderne featured the stylistic integration of architecture, furniture, murals, decorative elements, and mechanical services; both sought to unify art and craft within the material capabilities of modern, serial production.

Few buildings illustrate the Art Deco and Streamline styles better than movie palaces of the late 1920s and early 1930s, as well as smaller theaters built after the Depression. While all of the leading movie palace architects experimented with Deco themes, some did so more successfully than others. The most celebrated Deco movie palace is the Paramount in Oakland, California, designed by Timothy Pflueger and constructed in 1931. The Paramount demonstrates the tendency of movie palace architects to introduce modern elements without sacrificing the lyrical quality of classical ornament. The use of allegorical murals, highly stylized statuary, brilliant color, and intricately patterned geometric decor retained much of the heroic scale, vertical line, romance, and fantasy of earlier theaters.

In addition to their artistry, Deco and Moderne demonstrated clear economic advantage over their design predecessors. Originating as a response to mass production and the age of the machine, Deco interiors were generally less elaborate and less labor-intensive—and therefore less costly—than other designs. Additionally, the rising interest in abstract geometrics no doubt influenced the development of a lower, rectangular hall and shallow balcony for the palaces of the late 1920s.

SOUND AND THE RESTRUCTURING OF EMPIRE

Sound arrived in 1927. Although corporate mergers and competition continued to characterize the struggle for Hollywood domination, the development of the "talkies" dealt all of the major players a new hand. According to film industry historian Douglas Gomery, the arrival of sound at once influenced all three spheres—film production, distribution, and the theaters themselves—of the Hollywood enterprise. (26) Production and screenplays were tailored to support a new type of movie star, an actor or actress who could sing, dance, and talk. Distribution experts who influenced the apportionment of projection equipment leapt at a fresh opportunity to control profits that the audio phenomenon would undoubtedly generate. Theaters not wired for sound were left with little opportunity to compete. More significantly, the concept of augmented entertainment—live stage shows, organs, and orchestras—faced a near-total eclipse. No longer was there need to build elaborate theaters with full stage facilities. The quality of film as entertainment became more human with the advent of sound. The intensity of the film experience now could rival that of live performance. With the advent of sound, film itself was the marketed product, and stage productions were no longer needed as a promotional tool.

When the dust that followed the sound explosion settled, as Professor Gomery notes, the smaller regional exhibition empires (with which larger corporations had quarreled throughout the early days of monopoly) were absorbed by the giant film companies. (27) By 1929, Hollywood had reached the peak of its consolidation. Five vertically integrated companies in varying states of merger—Loew's, Paramount, Warner Bros. Pictures, Fox, and RKO—entered the Depression on the crest of the film industry's first great decade of growth. Late in 1929, corporations began to spend less on elaborate theaters, and movie palaces constructed after that year reflected the more conservative financial outlays with restraint in both design and size.

The year 1929 proved as important to American design as to American economics. It was in that year that Alfred H. Barr established New York's Museum of Modern Art. Throughout Europe—in Germany, by the Bauhaus, in Holland, by DeStijl, and in France, by Le Corbusier—the canons of design expression were being fundamentally rewritten. In 1932, Henry Russell Hitchcock and Philip Johnson popularized the phrase International Style (formerly termed the Modern Movement) and codified its existence in the United States with an exhibition they curated at the Museum of Modern Art. The monograph accompanying the exhibition was widely read, and modern design—with its cost-saving technology, new materials, and austere geometry—was released into the main current of America's commercial and industrial imagination.

The same conduits that had embraced the imagery of eclecticism were quick to disclaim it. Architectural journals, the popular press, and fashion magazines all seemed to form a new consensus. The June 1934 issue of *Architectural Record* extolled the merits of "modernization," and in a featured article architect Ben Schlanger argued that elaborate theaters were inefficient and obsolete. Restricted construction, the coming of sound, shifting neighborhood populations, new technology, favorable acoustical shape, minimum initial investment, and generally lower costs were among 20 reasons listed for encouraging the design of smaller theaters. (28) Ornate downtown showcases became a monument to the past, and new theaters for film incorporated the stripped-down look of the International Style. The exaggerated use of architectural ornament was no longer appropriate in the smaller, post-1934 movie houses.

MOVIE PALACE ARCHITECTS

The leading theater architects of Hollywood's Golden Era generated designs commensurate with the enthusiasm of commissioners who parlayed large brick and mortar budgets into huge profits. Thomas Lamb, C.W. Rapp and George L. Rapp, and John Eberson—architects whose work was distin-

The grand foyer of Rapp and Rapp's 1921 Tivoli Theatre in Chicago, with its ornate coffered ceiling, crystal chandeliers, and murals, was patterned after the Chapelle Royale at Versailles.

guished by the combination of marketing strategy, invention, and romance—yielded the criteria against which hundreds of exhibitors measured their structural investments. These architects, like many others who designed movie palaces, earned their credentials in the service of vaudeville. Most had completed theaters before the advent of the motion picture industry and its subsequent domination of the downtown entertainment district. Connections to show business, as well as a practical understanding of theater environment and technology, became for them the basis of new opportunity, and inevitably the signatures of leading movie palace architects became associated with local, regional, and, in a few cases, national theater chains.

Lamb's career carried him from Scotland to New York, where his first significant theater commissions were executed. Before designing the Regent in 1913, he produced several vaudeville halls for circuits operating in the Northeast, a network soon enveloped by the expansion of the film industry. Lamb's architectural vocabulary was rooted in his early appreciation of the neoclassical designs of Robert Adam, the highly respected 18th-century British architect. With changing fashions and intensified competition, however, Lamb steadily expanded his palette, blending Palladian, baroque, rococo, and Art Deco elements. Although his best known project, the 1928 Ohio Theater in Columbus, was more grand than his earlier work, his eclectic orchestration of detail was still characterized by elegance and equilibrium.

Examples of Thomas Lamb's work were acquired by Marcus Loew in his take-over of the Poli vaudeville chain, for which Lamb had designed several northeastern theaters. Lamb's relationship with the Loew's organization resulted in numerous commissions throughout the country, particularly in the mid-Atlantic and eastern regions. Lamb died in 1942, having produced many of the nation's greatest movie palaces, including landmarks in several major American cities, as well as buildings in England, Australia, North Africa, India, and Egypt.

Cornelius Ward Rapp was already an established architect with field experience in theater design when his younger brother, George, moved to Chicago to join him in the creation of one of the country's most respected movie palace practices. Although they frequently experimented with images from different historical periods and regional styles, including many Spanish, Italian, Moorish, and Art Deco renderings, the Rapps developed several recurring trademarks influenced by a visit to Paris early in their career. Among these were the triumphal arch (usually in the form of the facade's central window), the monumental staircase (fashioned after that in Charles Garnier's 1875 Paris Opera), and the grand, column-lined lobby (often recalling the Hall of Mirrors at Versailles).

Perhaps the best example among architect/movie chain associations of Hollywood's Golden Era is that of Rapp and Rapp and Chicago's largest exhibitor, Balaban and Katz. The Rapp Brothers began their long relationship with the chain in 1917 with construction of their first large theater, the Central

A fanciful Chicago creation by John Eberson: the 1925 Capitol Theatre. The auditorium, with its ceiling murals and statuary recalling a classical garden, was typical of the open-air illusion that enhanced Eberson's romantic atmospherics.

Park. With the success of the Central Park and its immediate successor, the Riviera (1919), Rapp and Rapp became "architects by appointment to Balaban and Katz," and went on to design Chicago's most elaborate movie palaces. When the Balaban and Katz empire was absorbed by Paramount in 1926, Adolph Zukor installed Sam Katz as head of the Publix-Paramount operation. The Rapps were Katz's natural choice for many new Publix-Paramount theaters, which spread from New York to Portland, Oregon, as Katz expanded the empire.

Few movie palace architects were as aggressively theatrical in their designs as John Eberson, pioneer of the atmospheric auditorium. In 1923, Eberson overturned conventional movie palace methodology with the completion of the Majestic Theatre in Houston. He replaced the ornate ceiling domes of the traditional European theater format with a smooth plaster shell painted deep blue and perforated by hundreds of twinkling pinpoint lights. A projector hidden in the sidewalls animated the surface of the ceiling with slowly moving clouds. The outdoor theme permitted Eberson to explore a bold and altogether unconventional approach to the design of auditorium sidewalls. Mediterranean images were combined to create outdoor courtyards of exotic fantasy and romance, an appropriate setting for the fiction on screen. Eberson's illusions were designed to recall an idealized village, complete with windows, rooftops, embellished doors and walls, exotic plants, and birds perched or suspended in flight above the audience.

Many architects, including Lamb and the Rapp Brothers, experimented with atmospheric auditoriums, although Eberson's work held title to the concept. Like Lamb, Eberson began by working with a local southwestern exhibitor, the Hoblitzelle chain in Texas. (29) The success and popularity of Eberson's atmospheric-style theater, however, led to projects for numerous companies throughout the South and Midwest, and Eberson can be safely credited with inspiring—at least in part—the explosion of exotic designs in the late 1920s.

In addition to Thomas Lamb, the Rapp brothers, and John Eberson, other architects working in the 1920s contributed to the development and stylization of movie palaces. On the West Coast, B. Marcus Priteca established a longstanding relationship with the Pantages chain. Priteca, who continued to design theaters well into the 1930s, left his imprint on nearly 500 cinemas. G. Albert Landsburgh applied his Beaux Arts education to several theater projects in California and the western states, including Salt Lake City's Capital, San Francisco's Golden Gate, and Los Angeles' Orpheum. Landsburgh's exquisite details reflect his early influence by European classical, gothic, and renaissance architecture.

The Boller Brothers of Kansas City contracted for several exhibitors throughout Missouri, Kansas, New Mexico, Texas, and the Southwest. Like Priteca, the Bollers adopted a variety of exotic and regional themes for their designs, producing theaters as diverse as the KiMo in Albuquerque (with its native American motif), and the Missouri in St. Joseph, en-

The Chicago Theatre, a Rapp and Rapp design for the Balaban and Katz chain, with its triumphal center arch—a hallmark of the architects.

Crowds gather at the Oakland Paramount for a gala motion picture premiere.

crusted with a Spanish baroque facade. C. Howard Crane, who worked out of Detroit for the Fox circuit, was well-versed in the classical vocabulary and in later years designed with exuberant ornamentation.

Lesser known but important architecture firm/theater chain relationships also include Hoffman and Henon for the East Coast's Stanley operation and Levy and Klein for Chicago's Marks Brothers. Several other firms—J.E.O. Pridmore and Mayger and Graven in the Midwest, Weeks and Day, S. Charles Lee, and Timothy Pflueger in California, and W.W. Ahlschlager, who designed New York's Roxy as well as several large Chicago theaters—deserve mention. Nearly all of these architects utilized precedents established in the work of the true deans of movie palace architecture—Lamb, Rapp and Rapp, and Eberson.

GROWTH WITHOUT CONSTRUCTION, THEN DECLINE

In the years from 1934 to 1960, the movie industry experienced a period of recovery from the Depression followed by rapid growth, albeit without accompanying movie theater construction. Hollywood found the Depression years costly

but not incapacitating. It has been estimated that between 1931 and 1933 movie corporations suffered a 25 to 40 percent decline in revenues, but fully recovered the loss by the start of World War II. (30)

The most lucrative period in the history of Hollywood occurred between 1940 and 1946, when old downtown theaters were alive again briefly with full houses and full-length films. Americans at home participated in the war effort by going to movie theaters. Newsreels broadcast official information on the latest defeats and victories in the Pacific, African, and European theaters of war, and the movie theater was to World War II what home television was to the Vietnam War. War bonds also were sold at theaters, and screen stars made personal appearances to promote bond sales. In 1946, the best year in the history of the industry, over four billion tickets were sold. (31)

The economic boom of the war years proved a short-lived happiness for Hollywood. In the famous 1948 Paramount Case (U.S. v. Paramount et al.), the U.S. Supreme Court held that the eight major Hollywood corporations were to divest their brick and mortar holdings—the movie theaters themselves—in the United States. The corporations' long-fought financial control of production, distribution, and exhibition of films was dismantled.

Between 1947 and 1955, the rise of television led to a series of attempts by Hollywood to reinvigorate its product and

The Capital Court, a suburban Milwaukee movie theater constructed in the late 1950s.

recoup audiences lost to suburban sprawl. America's flight to the suburbs had a catastrophic affect on urban theaters, and between 1948 and 1970, the number of indoor screens in use in the United States dropped nearly 50 percent. (32) CinemaScope, 3-D movies, Cinerama, and even "Sensurround" were among the devices introduced to do battle with TV, and conversion to 70mm projection is responsible for the stage modifications (including widening the procenium arch to accept new and wider screens) found in many older theaters.

EPILOGUE AND PREFACE

A new appreciation of the past in the late 1960s and early 1970s, reinforced by the United States Bicentennial in 1976, helped to foster the climate in which historic preservation emerged as a popular cause. Adaptive reuse, neighborhood conservation, the restoration arts, and a high regard for historical allusion in new design have now been fully integrated into the economic and practical vocabularies of American architects.

The legacy of the movie palace is being transmitted to an architecture of entertainment that has applied a similar formula to different commercial enterprises. Disney World and the neon-filled nights of Las Vegas casinos, urban "marketplaces," and department stores with their "street of boutiques" equally insulate and remove customers from the "ordinary" world. (33) Like the movie palaces, these "colonies of Hollywood" entertain by transforming the total environment into an architecture of illusion and escape. (34)

At a time when the movie palace is undergoing a renaissance, the future of the cinema as a public event is in doubt. A front-page headline in the August 19, 1981, issue of *The Wall Street Journal* spelled out bad news for Hollywood: "Coming Attractions: With Ticket Sales Off, Some Movie Exhibitors Project a Bleak Future; Cable TV and Videocassettes Are Two Reasons Cited for Screens to Go Dark." (35)

Expanded home entertainment possibilities threaten to undermine not only stageless theaters but also the very sociology of "going out to the movies." To compound the crisis, Harvard Business School professor Theodore Levitt suggests, the moviegoing age-group (18-35) is diminishing. (36) Beyond these factors, experts agree that the movie industry image has not been helped by the proliferation of small, multiplex cinemas, box-like theaters with meager screens and the most basic decor. Ironically, Hollywood's best-selling pictures are led by the recent wave of epic science fiction fantasies which feature sensory extravaganza—extraterrestrial themes, eight-track stereo sound, and nonstop special effects. In a word, these productions employ the same formula used by movie

The Belmont, a Chicago movie palace designed by W. W. Ahlschlager, was reused as a bowling alley. The theater is now dark, presenting yet another challenge for renaissance.

palace planners. They transform worlds, providing the patron with a sense of removal from the commonplace.

The suburban cinemas that virtually wiped out the downtown movie palace now stand at the threshold of a comparable disaster. Hardly the white elephant most critics thought it might become, the large downtown theater has proved an urban asset. Its identity, its value as an architectural "event," its connection to the past, and its utility in cost-conscious urban redevelopment scenarios have led dozens of cities to invest in its renaissance.

Despite their renewed popularity and acknowledged role as important community assets, America's movie palaces continue to face several serious threats. For instance, the restoration of a community's grandest downtown palaces may draw recognition away from smaller theaters with similar historic interest and reuse potential. Such "forgotten" theaters face not only continued neglect and deterioration, but also the ultimate threat of demolition before the community can rally to save them.

On the other hand, a theater may be well on its way to reuse when bad luck strikes, threatening its new life. In Manchester, New Hampshire, the Palace Theatre, meticulously restored for use as a performing arts resource, sustained extensive damage when water pipes froze and burst in 1981. The theater's future remains in doubt.

Older movie theaters are also threatened by inappropriate reuse or renovation. An extreme example of inappropriate reuse is a multi-story parking garage built within the shell of a Detroit theater. More common, however, is the imposition of detail, lighting, color, or other construction in a style sharply in contrast to that of the original theater design, yet billed as "restoration."

Finally, there is the question of funding for the renaissance and reuse of movie palaces. The vast majority of theater adaptive use projects were started in the 1970s, a period of unprecedented support for the arts. A number of Federal programs and legislation, such as block grants, special incentives built into the Tax Reform Act of 1976, and programs administered by the National Endowment for the Arts, helped assist, encourage, or underwrite the restoration or reprogramming of dozens of movie theaters. With major changes in Federal fiscal policy, communities that otherwise relied on government funding must now look elsewhere for capital and operating assistance.

Despite a new economic climate and other challenges outlined here, the same imagination that already has rescued movie palaces across the country will no doubt identify and create new ways to integrate national heritage and art with business and economics. Strengthened by their symbolic and practical value, immunized against the threat of the next media revolution, movie palaces promise to withstand each new test of time, witnesses to history come full circle.

REAL DREAMS

MOTIVATIONS FOR MOVIE PALACE REUSE

While the two catalysts in movie palace reuse are the sponsor and the facility itself, motivations for the projects are many and varied. Sponsors differ from case to case, as do the characteristics, conditions, and circumstances that surround the facility in which the sponsor has an interest.

Sponsors can be local citizens concerned with preserving their community's architectural heritage or owners of older theaters who initiate the search for new use. Sponsors can also be private or not-for-profit groups, profit making management or development companies, or city governments. Whichever the theater restoration sponsor may be, that individual or organization usually remains a part of the decision-making process, whether or not that process leads to the formation of a group to oversee and operate the project and its property.

In the business of movie palace reuse, the relationship between sponsor and facility is most easily defined in terms of needs. As profiled in this report, among the most common reasons a sponsor and a facility come together are that a user needs a facility, a facility needs a user, or a city needs a redevelopment anchor.

A user needs a facility

In St. Louis, for example, the decision to renovate and adapt a large movie palace occurred after other alternatives, including new construction and the adaptation of other types of older buildings, had been explored and analyzed. The St. Louis Symphony needed a home—an elegant, acoustically superior concert hall with adjacent administrative space, storage areas, and dressing rooms. Restoring a movie palace satisfied both needs and budget constraints.

Show business in general has recognized the potential of restored movie palaces. The Nederlander-Shorenstein organization found that the Golden Gate Theatre in San Francisco —and more than 20 other movie palaces nationwide— answered its need for first-rate houses on the Broadway touring show circuit.

Private investors involved in fields other than show business also have found that movie palaces offer an attractive combination of space and decorative ornamentation. For instance, the Century Mall in Chicago—a reused theater—is an enclosed retail shopping center with a spiraling, seven-level ramp of boutiques overlooking an eight-story atrium. In a Cleveland suburb, the Beachcliff Mall—also a reused theater —offers a two-floor shopping complex within a tiered stagehouse. In both cases, the external characteristics of the theater were left unchanged. Other movie theater invest-

(*Preceding page*) Elaborate Spanish baroque ornamentation in the Ohio Theatre auditorium.

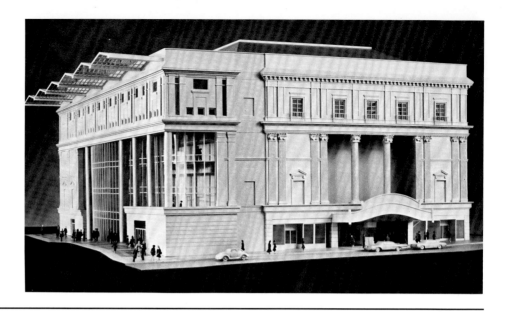

ments include nightclubs and restaurants. Less conventional and more controversial private investment adaptations include a complex of racquetball courts in St. Louis and a gymnasium in New York.

Movie palaces also enjoy new life as homes to religious and educational groups. In Winston-Salem, the North Carolina School for the Performing Arts is transforming a movie theater, providing not only NCSPA students but an entire community with a new cultural resource.

A facility needs a user

In Columbus, Ohio, a group of theater organ enthusiasts collected their resources and energies to prevent the imminent demolition of the Ohio Theatre. Early efforts led to the formation of a not-for-profit sponsoring corporation, the Columbus Association for the Performing Arts, which subsequently demonstrated that the historic facility could satisfy the city's need for a multiple-purpose arts facility. Fundraising, volunteer support, and practical marketing strategies contributed to the rescue of what is now a National Historic Landmark and the official theater of the State of Ohio.

In Macon, Georgia, the Grand Opera House—once host to Sarah Bernhardt and Will Rogers but, in 1967, dark and unsafe for occupancy—was eyed for demolition so that a parking lot could be constructed. Concerned citizens established the Macon Arts Council to save and restore the opera house and other local historic structures. Today, the Grand is once again host to local and internationally known artists, its restoration honored by the American Association for State and Local History.

A city needs a redevelopment anchor

Faced with the fallout from the 1950s and '60s urban flight to suburbia, downtowns from coast to coast and in most points in between have recognized the valuable role movie palaces can play in drawing new customers to aging business districts.

In terms of sheer magnitude, Cleveland's Playhouse Square leads the myriad theater reuse projects nationwide, and a recent study reveals that the restoration and careful reprogramming of its cluster of theaters have brought jobs, business, patrons, and money back into the heart of the city. The revitalization of San Antonio's downtown movie theater/performing arts district promises to do much the same for the Texas city. In Madison, years of controversy over the location of a long overdue civic center ended when the city purchased a downtown movie theater and adjacent retail space, transforming the structures into a cultural "crossroads."

Two views of the architect's model for proposed addition to the Ohio Theatre, Columbus. The design features a glass-enclosed pavilion and roofed esplanade walk for patrons.

MULTIPLE-PURPOSE PERFORMING ARTS CENTERS

The kaleidoscope of contemporary performing arts has helped generate the development of facilities that can accommodate diverse programming requirements. From the grand scale production of opera and ballet to the lesser demands of chamber music and modern jazz, one theater can offer the requisite stage and wing space and such technology as sound and light boards and complex fly lofts. The economic advantages of multiple use are that for a single investment, and with centralized management, a large and diverse arts audience can be effectively served. The following case studies profile the technical and patron-related adaptations of movie palaces to satisfy the broadest possible constituency.

The art of saving a movie palace

OHIO THEATRE, COLUMBUS, OHIO

Volunteer action saved the Ohio Theatre in Columbus and is working piece by piece to restore it. Little more than the will of a community intervened 12 years ago to prevent the

waste of an undervalued urban asset. Today, the 1928 masterwork of architect Thomas Lamb is not only the official theater of the State of Ohio, but it is also one of only three movie palaces to be declared a National Historic Landmark. The restored Ohio Theatre provides an elegant home for the Columbus Symphony and Ballet Metropolitan, and its performing arts calendar is one of the most diversified in the United States.

The achievement of the Columbus Association for the Performing Arts (CAPA), established in 1969 to choreograph the race against the wrecker's ball, represents the consolidated efforts of hundreds of citizens who have contributed thousands of dollars in time and talent to the restoration effort. Less than 10 years after saving the theater from demolition, CAPA was able to boast 329 arts events at the Ohio in a single year. In addition, in 1980 Ohio audiences (who represented a 22 percent increase over the preceding year) generated a substantial economic contribution to downtown Columbus: of more than 458,260 attendees in 1980, local patrons contributed $2.90 per capita and out-of-town patrons contributed $14.40 per capita. (37) Today, the renaissance of downtown Columbus can in part be credited to the success of the Ohio.

ACQUISITION: THE $1.75-MILLION ALTERNATIVE
Efforts to save the Ohio began with a small group of theater

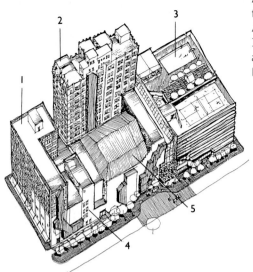

Architect's drawing of component structures for the proposed San Antonio Performing Arts Center (left). Legend: 1, Brady Building; 2, Majestic Theatre Building; 3, parking garage and retail space; 4, Galleria with restaurant; 5, Empire Theatre Building.

The palatial scarlet and gold auditorium of the restored Ohio Theatre in Columbus (right). Painted gold stars sparkle on the sounding board above the ornate proscenium arch.

and theater organ enthusiasts whose initial struggle led to the formation of CAPA. After the acoustical promise of the theater was tested and confirmed, more than $1.75 million in personal loans, guarantees, and contributions from local individuals and institutions was needed to purchase and rehabilitate the theater. A core group of prominent Columbus citizens, including lawyers, developers, architects, and business executives, were successful in the drive to secure the necessary monies to buy the Ohio Theatre, and all of its fixtures and equipment, as well as the adjacent Grand Theatre. CAPA received nonprofit status from the Internal Revenue Service, and an intensive communitywide fundraising campaign was launched to restore the facilities.

In only six months, mortgages for both theaters had been secured, and CAPA's task shifted to demonstrating the theater's potential for satisfying the city's need for a performing arts facility. Volunteers set about to clean, repair, and reequip the theater—which seats nearly 2,900—in order to put it into service immediately. Performances took place amidst the slow restoration. Operating funds of $100,000, raised in the early campaign, were quickly depleted, but the enthusiasm and continuing efforts of unpaid staff and key community supporters led to a series of critical matching grants that kept the incipient organization afloat.

ORGANIZATIONAL STRUCTURE AND PHASED DEVELOPMENT
Five themes characterize CAPA's current success, strategy,

and future goals:

□ restoration projects undertaken, as funds become available, in conjunction with a long-range plan that addresses patron safety, areas necessary for use of the theater as a performing arts center, patron comfort, and theater aesthetics—in that order

□ voluntarism

□ authenticity of restoration

□ new construction, including stage expansion, the creation of a new pavilion to the east of the theater, and installation of systems necessary to facilitate state-of- the-art multi-use performance capability

□ ongoing fundraising campaigns, diversified year-round programming, and expanded services to the community.

The idea of well-focused, individual restoration projects and funding objectives is an invaluable public relations strategy. Whether the target of restoration is reseating or the replication of the original street lighting, each project acts to keep the community interested in the step-by-step development of the total program. Fund drives organized around specific goals also help to subdivide a large and sometimes vaguely defined amount of work into recognizable accomplishments. To date, this strategy has led to the completion of the gold-leaf repainting of the auditorium's east and west walls, installation of fire and smoke detectors, a new roof, a sound reinforcement system, restoration of the ticket kiosk at the entrance, and other projects. All restoration funds are

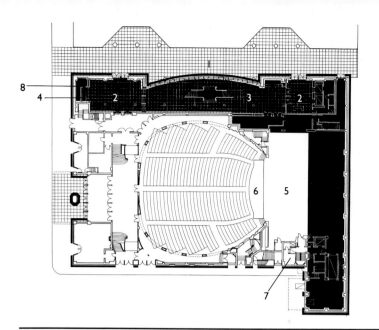

Architect's drawing of ground floor plan for the new Ohio Theatre addition. Legend: 1, esplanade; 2, entry; 3, lobby; 4, refreshments; 5, stage; 6, orchestra pit; 7, stage manager's office; 8, storage; 9, receiving.

raised specifically for restoration projects, and each step brings the Ohio closer to its goal of becoming a fully functional, authentically restored performing arts center.

In fulfilling the goals of its earliest feasibility study, CAPA is operating in the black. Government subsidy to the Ohio Theatre restoration and CAPA is minimal. Therefore, first-rate programming 52 weeks a year is critical to ensure the progress of the restoration. Notably, the Ohio has not turned its back on the movies. In fact, CAPA's summer film series has been a remarkably effective economic ballast from the start. Other income is derived from theater rentals, CAPA productions, contract services, membership dues, parking lot operation, operational grants, and concessions. The value of continuing volunteer support is unquantifiable, but the proportion of regular volunteers (who serve as ushers, concessionaires, and tour guides) to paid CAPA staff is roughly 24 to 1.

ARTS CENTER MANAGEMENT REQUIRES FULL-TIME STAFF

The management of a large performing arts center with a fully booked calendar and ongoing building improvements is a demanding task. CAPA's operation in 1981 required a full-time staff of 16, including an executive director; assistant director for public relations; director of building, restoration, and grants; audience development director; stage manager; and resident organist. In fact, CAPA management expenses represent its largest single expenditures. The CAPA staff is governed by 30 nonsalaried members of the board of trust-

ees who determine policy and programs, and raise funds. The board of trustees is augmented by 10 committees, each with specific responsibilities.

The ongoing restoration of the Ohio Theatre has earned a multitude of awards, citations, and legislative recognitions. The vitality of the project is in large part the product of a professional organization that manages every stage of development. No doubt, Ohio Theatre-watchers nationwide are as eager to applaud the theater's final phase of restoration as are the local patrons who will benefit from the amenities the theater brings to their region.

Community-wide support in the Northwest

5TH AVENUE THEATRE, SEATTLE, WASHINGTON

Since the success of its 1962 World's Fair, Seattle has enjoyed a growing population and thriving downtown retail community embellished by the revitalized Pike Marketplace. Unlike Providence, Pittsburgh, St. Louis, Cleveland, and other cities of comparable population, Seattle's experiment with movie palace reuse derived from the regional need for a first-rate multipurpose theater equipped to accommodate road shows and touring Broadway productions.

Now the Pacific Northwest enjoys just such a facility in the 5th Avenue, a movie palace masterpiece located in the heart of Seattle's central business district. Restored in conjunction

Seattle's 5th Avenue Theatre, with its oriental motif inspired by the city's 19th-century China Trade.

with a multi-use retail development, the reprogramming and renovation of the 5th Avenue involves an unusual team of players, significantly independent of any federal, state, or public funding.

OFFICE/RETAIL/THEATER COMPLEX

The 5th Avenue was originally constructed as a part of The Skinner Building, an eight-story office/retail/theater complex. The theater operated as a movie house until it went dark in 1976. At that time, UNICO, a Seattle property management and development firm, was beginning work on the new Rainier Square retail mall development beneath The Skinner Building. In addition to developing Rainier Square, UNICO manages The Skinner Building, so the firm began to explore alternative uses for the movie palace.

The first feasibility study explored a variety of development scenarios, including conversion to triplex cinema, retail shops, and a Chinese restaurant. The most attractive proposal was for a multi-use performing arts facility that would satisfy the need for a quality road show theater to serve Seattle's growing arts audiences. Far less expensive than a new theater, the adaptation would also serve to rejuvenate one of the West Coast's finest movie palaces, already listed on the National Register of Historic Places.

Once UNICO determined that a multi-use performing arts facility was the most appropriate direction to pursue, its task was to generate funds to support theater renovation. David

Skinner, president of the Skinner Corporation and a long-standing Seattle arts advocate, collaborated with others to establish the not-for-profit 5th Avenue Theatre Association. In a fundraising grand slam, the group was able to secure in only 10 days $100,000 to $200,000 in loan guarantees from 43 local corporations and businesses. Each guarantor in turn became a founder of the 5th Avenue Theatre Association. With a $2.6-million loan fully underwritten, UNICO retained an architectural firm to begin the theater restoration.

Seattle's port-of-call and maritime connection to the Orient influenced R. C. Reamer in 1926 to design the 5th Avenue as an oriental palace inspired by images of the Forbidden City of Peking. The carefully researched decor includes oversized round columns that punctuate vibrant patterns painted in muted shades of blue, gold, crimson, and black, accented by green and white trim. Decorative elements are inlaid. The orchestra's sidewalls are set into columns framing intricate silhouettes that recall the art of oriental paper cutting and depict a variety of mythical figures and legendary animals.

The architect who oversaw the 5th Avenue renovation was R. F. McCann, who had proposed the adaptive use of movie palaces in a paper presented to the Washington chapter of the American Institute of Architects several years before the campaign was launched to restore the Seattle facility. McCann's approach began with item-by-item alternatives for rehabilitation, thus allowing for the most efficient allocation of available funds. He separated the two principal

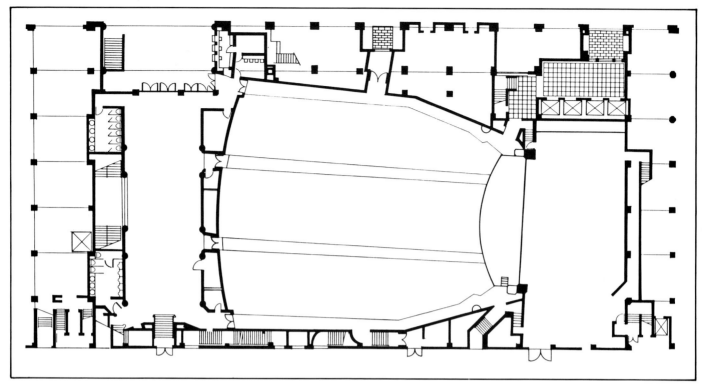

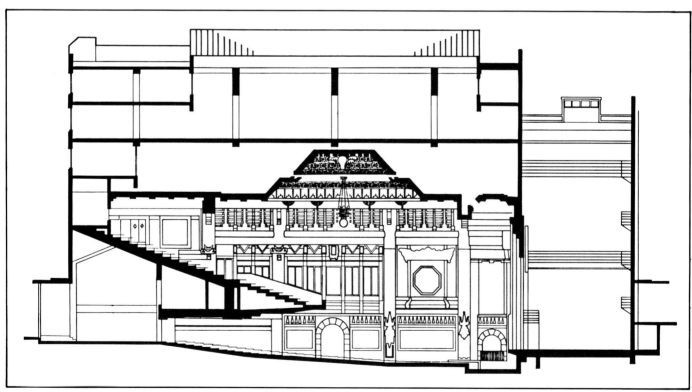

Architect's drawings of 5th Avenue Theatre,
Seattle: floor plan (top) and longitudinal section
(bottom) of house interior.

programmatic elements of the problem—the needs and comfort of the repeat-subscriber audience and those of touring stage productions—to isolate and clarify individual design issues. The resulting renovation program involved the following issues:

☐ patron comfort, improved seating redesigned for optimal sight lines, and upgraded lobby and ancillary amenities

☐ new, redesigned state-of-the-art stage facilities for touring companies and multiple-use performing arts, including ballet

☐ restoration of interior decor

☐ fully upgraded heating, ventilating, air conditioning, and electrical systems; fire and earthquake safety brought up to or exceeding code requirements

☐ refurbished and modernized lighting and acoustical systems.

The quality of the restoration was reiterated shortly before the grand reopening when the Heritage Conservation and Recreation Service, a federal agency, honored the theater project with a distinguished achievement award.

COOPERATION IS KEY

The cooperation of a not-for-profit performing arts association (representing many of Seattle's leading businesses, banks, corporations, foundations, and individuals), university, private development and property management company, and sensitive architect set the stage for the July 3, 1980, reopening of the 5th Avenue. Helen Hayes, Ethel Merman, and Merv

Griffin, as well as the Pacific Northwest Ballet, Seattle Opera, Seattle Repertory Company, and Seattle Symphony performed before a sellout crowd.

In its first season, the 5th Avenue Theatre Management Corporation, a not-for-profit subsidiary of UNICO Properties, Inc., recorded 34,000 subscribers. In its second season, it added another 2,000 regular patrons. Clearly, the response of the 5th Avenue's 43 initial founders and the general public foreshadowed the response of Seattle's citizens as well as the city's cultural vitality. The mixed-use development of the Rainier Square retail mall and the contiguous 5th Avenue Theatre—an outstanding achievement of the Seattle business community—serves as a valuable paradigm for other cities.

"It pays to play [an Art Deco gem]"

PARAMOUNT THEATRE, OAKLAND, CALIFORNIA

Oakland's Paramount Theatre, designed by architect Timothy L. Pflueger, is notable not only as an Art Deco masterpiece, but also because it was among the last great houses constructed before the Depression.

The Paramount operated as a movie theater from the time of its 1931 opening until 1970. At that time, Pflueger's architecture notwithstanding, the Paramount's fate was uncertain. Then, in a scenario similar to the one unfolding

The magnificent Art Deco auditorium (left) of the restored 1931 Oakland Paramount. Light projected from inside the proscenium columns gives the illusion of frosted glass, and red and gold lights play on the ceiling grille. In the lobby (right), the carpet is an exact copy of the six-color original. The Paramount's exuberant multi-colored terra-cotta facade (far right) illustrates opera, sports, dance, and circus themes.

with Powell Hall in St. Louis, the Oakland Symphony's search for a permanent home saved the theater from peril. The Paramount's auditorium was found to be acoustically excellent, the theater's price tag within the Symphony's budget, and the idea of preservation attractive. At a cost of $2 million, culled primarily from a fundraising campaign mounted specifically for that purpose, the Symphony acquired, restored, and upgraded the 3,000-seat facility.

After only nine months of reconstruction and repair under the supervision of the theater general manager and architects Skidmore, Owings, and Merrill (San Francisco) as consultants, the theater was reopened in fall 1973. The cooperation of the firm of the original architect's son, Milton T. Pflueger and Associates, helped to accomplish a standard-setting authenticity.

In the grand lobby, the four walls were scaffolded to the ceiling and loose dirt was blown down by compressed air. All surfaces were washed with an ammonia solution before being repainted in the original colors. In addition, the original amber and green incandescent lighting system, so important in bathing the walls and ceiling with bands of light, was restored.

In the auditorium, an elaborate lighting scheme discovered dismantled above the grilled ceiling was also restored. It once again controls the auditorium lights as well as the lights in the fluted metal strips comprising the proscenium columns. Light projected on the inside of the columns through the interleaved strips creates the effect of frosted glass.

Within the proscenium, both the valance and the main curtain were in place but unusable. Full-sized paper patterns were made from scraps, and new fabrics, dyed in New York, were assembled by a San Francisco stagehand specializing in theater restoration. The lobby carpet, as well as carpet in the rest of the house, is an exact copy of the six-color original. Three months were spent painstakingly repainting the murals in the smaller lounge areas. The upholstery fabrics in these public areas match almost exactly the originals they replace, and chairs and sofas, faithfully restored, have been returned to their original locations. In the auditorium, a three-month cleansing and repainting effort took place. The floral-patterned green and gold mohair seating upholstery, copied exactly from the original, was specifically manufactured for the Paramount.

Although the Oakland Symphony remains the Paramount's principal tenant, title to the restored theater was transferred by the Symphony to the city of Oakland in 1975. A not-for-profit corporation, Paramount Theatre of the Arts, Inc., was subsequently established to manage and operate the facility. Income is derived from rentals and bookings, including use for conventions and special events. Between 1973 and 1978, the Paramount played host to over 1,000 performances representing a diverse entertainment calendar. Since then, the average number of performances per year has increased. Total paid attendance was up 16 percent in 1979 over 1978, and ticket sales, over $1 million annually since 1975, grossed 51 percent greater in 1979 than in 1978. What factors account

The restored auditorium of the 1927 Brown Grand Theatre in Concordia, Kansas, with its proscenium and fire curtain painted with a scene of Napoleon at Waterloo. The theater's builder was Colonel Napoleon Bonaparte Brown.

for such box-office success? The answer is, in part, the Paramount itself—with its glorious Deco architecture—and, in part, aggressive marketing, alluded to in the Paramount management philosophy: It pays to play the Paramount. (38)

"Lend a hand to the Brown Grand"

BROWN GRAND THEATRE, CONCORDIA, KANSAS

With persistence, vision, widespread publicity, and expert fundraising, the Brown Grand Theatre in Concordia, Kansas, was restored to serve as a small, community-based performing arts resource. Built as an opera house in 1907 and adapted to exhibit film in 1925, the Brown Grand functioned as a movie theater until 1974. With its reopening in September 1980, Concordia townspeople celebrated both a transformed landmark and the 73rd anniversary of the Brown Grand's inaugural bill. Since the reopening, Concordia's 7,500 citizens have enjoyed a diverse calendar of activities that emphasize local arts, entertainment, and educational programming. Closely supervised by its 25-member board of directors, the 660-seat theater was reconceived as a civic and cultural entertainment center. In its first year of operation, the Brown Grand averaged better than one event per week, a ratio that is expected to increase.

INTEREST SPURRED BY TOWN CENTENNIAL
Initial interest in restoring the theater to its original condition germinated in the late 1960s, when townspeople were preparing for Concordia's centennial celebration. Local research enunciated the theater's significance, attracting the energies of several residents who quickly identified the opportunity to preserve one of the town's few remaining historic landmarks. At summer's end 1973, the Brown Grand was declared a National Historic Site. Less than a year later, it qualified for $10,000 in the federal government's Bicentennial matching grant funding program. This amount represented one-third of the total funds needed by the not-for-profit Brown Grand Opera House, Inc., to purchase the old theater.

After a community fundraising drive, the board (whose members had worked to have the theater declared a National Historic Site) was able to make the down payment on the theater on July 4, 1974, leaving another $500,000 to be raised for the restoration. Although a voter referendum that would have underwritten half of the project was defeated, the board of directors nonetheless prevailed. A professional fundraising group was retained by the board to oversee the second major fund drive, which netted $259,000 from donors willing to "lend a hand to the Brown Grand." Subsequently, $121,000 was procured through a series of three U.S. Department of Interior matching grants. A final campaign raised $100,000, enough in turn to raise the curtain on the Brown

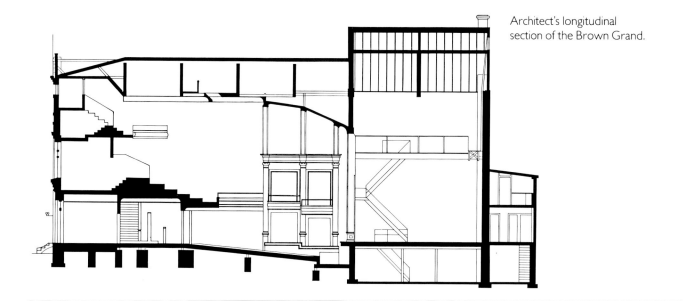

Architect's longitudinal
section of the Brown Grand.

Grand's renaissance. Contributions include gifts of more than $500 each from 137 institutions, individuals, organizations and businesses, and an even greater number of lesser donations.

MEDIA CAMPAIGN ASSISTS FUNDRAISING

Perhaps one key to Concordia's successful fundraising efforts, which resulted in approximately $67 per capita in needed monies, was the attention given the project by the statewide media. A public relations campaign was complemented by a 30-minute documentary film on the theater, funded by the Kansas Committee for the Humanities. *Behind the Grand Door* contained interviews with residents who remembered the theater's earlier days and no doubt helped to promote the successful campaign for restoration dollars.

Like many other citizen-organized restoration projects, the Brown Grand benefited from donated materials, services, and talent. In an unusual stroke of luck, nearby Bethany College contributed theater seats it no longer needed after purchasing new auditorium seating. Rehabilitated, the seats proved consistent in design and adequate for use in the Brown Grand.

Currently, operations and physical improvement revenues are needed to sustain the theater. An $8,900 subsidy provided by the city of Concordia paid the utility and insurance bills for the theater's first year, but that subsidy dropped to $5,400 in 1982. The board of directors is developing a package of funding strategies and events programming designed to attract continuing citizen support, and augment rental income.

The Brown Grand is currently managed and operated by the board, which meets monthly, other volunteers, and two part-time paid staff members who assist in administrative and custodial tasks. Despite limited funds the theater is supported by abundant enthusiasm. Its regular users include the Arts Council in Concordia, the local community college and high school, the Brown Grand Community Players, and the Concordia Community Concert Association. As a structure of architectural interest, the theater also attracts tour groups.

Whether through country and western music or Kansas University seminars, the Brown Grand is serving the people of Concordia and the entire north-central region of Kansas. The original builder, after whom the theater is named, constructed what he hoped would become an enduring cultural resource. His wish is being fulfilled. (39)

Kudos for a meticulous restoration

GRAND OPERA HOUSE, MACON, GEORGIA

In 1967, Macon's 80-year-old Grand Opera House sat dark, unsafe for occupancy. County titleholders were eyeing its

The crimson, gold, and white auditorium of Macon's restored Grand Opera House. The 1884 theater once boasted "the biggest stage south of the Mason-Dixon Line."

location with plans for a parking lot. Today, the Grand is one of the cultural focal points of this Georgia city, and local residents will usher in the theater's centennial with celebration.

Built in 1884 as the Academy of Music, the Grand then boasted the biggest stage south of the Mason-Dixon line. (Among the theater giants who performed there were Sarah Bernhardt, Lillian and Dorothy Gish, Maude Adams, George Burns and Gracie Allen, and Will Rogers.) Over the years, however, the 2,418-seat theater has known many transformations. In 1905 the Academy owners replaced architect Alexander Blair's facade with a seven-story office building and renamed the theater the Grand Opera House. Less than 15 years later, motion picture equipment was installed. A gradual decline in revenues led to disrepair and in 1964 the theater was closed.

In 1967 the Bibb County Commission, which held title to the theater, made plans to demolish it in favor of a parking lot. In response to this threat to Macon's architectural heritage, three community activists established the Macon Arts Council. The group's mission was to save and restore an eminently reusable historic facility. The following year the commission approved the council's alternative plans for the theater. The council's campaign was fortified by an alliance of civic groups whose members were enlisted to help raise badly needed restoration funds. Priority improvements included a new roof, new rigging for the eight-story fly loft, a reconditioned surface for the 58 by 90-foot stage, and a deepened orchestra

pit. In addition, the theater interior was completely refurbished. Replicas of original fixtures, velvet hangings, chandeliers, and bent-back chairs for the box seating embellished the theater's restored color scheme and ornamentation. The Grand's meticulous restoration was duly honored by the American Association for State and Local History, and it is worthy of note that every cent of the $345,000 undertaking can be credited to donations from the people of Macon.

The Grand reopened to a full house on April 6, 1970. Its first renaissance season brought both local and internationally known recitalists, orchestras, and other performers to the stage and 65,000 patrons to the theater. The Macon Arts Council pursues a broad, inclusive programming philosophy for the Grand. Most importantly, though, the Grand remains a community theater, a Macon institution dedicated to the people of the city that rallied around it. (40)

Out of the ashes

CAPITOL THEATRE, YAKIMA, WASHINGTON

A campaign to restore and recycle the Capitol Theatre in Yakima, Washington, as a performing arts center had been waged and won when the 1920s vaudeville/movie showcase was nearly lost to fire. The blaze occurred in August 1975, shortly before the start of the reprogrammed facility's 1975-76

Stone and masonry facade of Tacoma's Capitol Theatre (above), on which symbolic lyres rest atop the pediments in each of five arches. The artist of the Capitol Theatre's original ceiling dome murals assisted in the design and decoration of the new Capitol auditorium (right).

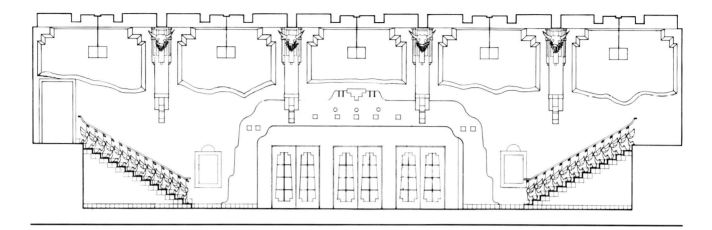

season. The Capitol's interior was totally destroyed. Its owner, the city of Yakima, and its principal tenant, the Capitol Theatre Committee, were left with little more than a charred structural shell.

Before the fire, the demand for a performing arts center to serve Yakima (population 40,000) and the central Washington area had already been established. Likewise, it had been agreed that the Capitol was an invaluable landmark, well-suited to support multiple-purpose arts programming. Amid the smoldering potential of the original theater, only one question remained: should the city and its people build anew or should they reconstruct the old?

CITIZENS CALL FOR REBUILDING

The city immediately retained the Capitol Committee as its consultant, charging it with preparing a feasibility study to explore and clarify alternatives. Citizens were polled, construction experts consulted, and costs for alternative options weighed. In 10 weeks the committee appeared before the city council with its emphatic recommendation: the Capitol should be rebuilt. The council responded by asking a local architect to develop design proposals and cost estimates for the reconstruction. The architect's subsequent $2.2-million proposal indicated the no-frills concept of the facility. (41)

After insurance monies and recoverable building structure were deducted, the city and the Capitol Theatre Committee faced a $1.2-million price tag. The city council agreed to split the difference, challenging the Capitol Theatre Trust, off-

spring of the Theatre Committee, with raising $600,000 in publicly donated reconstruction funds. Shortly after the first anniversary of the fire, the fund's appeal through local media generated the necessary dollars and the city council reciprocated in kind.

Phase One reconstruction of a "minimally functional theatre" was started in November 1976. Inflation and funds estimated for Phase Two, a historically accurate reconstruction of the original Capitol Theatre, added nearly $2 million to the committee's challenge. Together, owner and tenant explored funding sources beyond the immediate community, and funding proposals to Yakima County and the U.S. Economic Development Administration were successful.

A MODERNIZED FACSIMILE

The additional funds allowed the Capitol Committee's architects to work toward an entirely modernized, updated facsimile of the old theater. Color photographs of the original interior enabled specialists to model plaster and fiberglass replicas of original ornaments. Thousands of individual elements, manufactured in a temporary factory set up near the construction site, were produced and installed. The architects were able to locate and retain the artist of the original ceiling dome murals, and at the age of 81 he contributed significantly to the design of the Capitol's redecoration.

Theater seats, acquired from the old Constitution Hall in Washington, D.C., were reupholstered and installed in the continental fashion (no center aisle) by the same firm partici-

Architect's drawing of lobby walls in Albuquerque's KiMo Theatre. Note buffalo head column capitals of north wall (left), and exotic native American Indian bird motif on staircase railing of south wall (right).

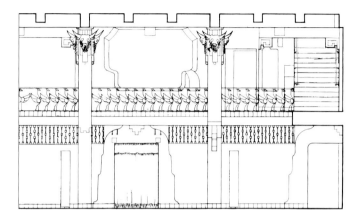

pating in the Paramount Theater restoration in Aurora, Illinois. In addition, a new steel and poured concrete orchestra floor was constructed over 7,000 sq. ft. of badly needed auxiliary space.

The Capitol's lower-level area includes administrative offices as well as a rentable lobby and meeting hall. Like the rest of the theater, the area benefits from independently controlled zone heating and air conditioning supplied by a new mechanical plant located on the stagehouse roof. State-of-the-art stage, sound, and lighting systems can accommodate a variety of production requirements.

Three years after the smoke from the 1975 fire cleared, Yakima celebrated the return of the all new "Grand Old Lady" with a month of diverse grand opening events. Sharing the November 1978 opening month calendar were comedian Bob Hope, the Yakima Symphony, the Philadelphia String Quartet, Yakima Public Schools, guitarist/singer Jose Feliciano, and Lawrence Welk's Champagne Music Family. The first full season offered lectures, concerts, touring Broadway productions, opera, choral groups, country and western music, repertory theater, ballet, and jazz.

The Capitol Theatre Corporation had an opportunity to clarify its programming policies after the 1975 fire. A public opinion poll conducted in conjunction with the post-fire feasibility study indicated a desire for a community-based performing arts and entertainment center that would serve the entire central Washington region. Residents of Yakima contributed almost one-fifth of the Capitol Reconstruction funds,

and their continued enthusiasm is now evident in response to theater programming. Theater events have proven to be a highly reliable source of revenue, a measure not only of good management and first-rate facilities, but also of the Capitol's close contact with the city's 40,000 residents.

American Indian motif in the Southwest

KIMO THEATRE, ALBUQUERQUE, NEW MEXICO

Albuquerque's KiMo Theatre is one of the few movie palaces to feature a native American Indian motif. Prior to designing the theater, Carl and Robert Boller, well-known cinema architects of the West and Midwest, spent several months in New Mexico collecting images and ideas for the Albuquerque theater. The resulting decor includes an assortment of references to Pueblo, Zuni, and Navaho artifacts, with rich color schemes and adobe surfaces mirroring the palette of the southwestern desert.

Opened in 1927, the KiMo operated continuously until March 1980, when it was closed for the first phase of a renovation that will transform it into a small multiple-purpose performing arts resource. The City of Albuquerque gained title to the theater several years prior to the beginning of the restoration effort, and it is with city monies, as well as a grant from the U.S. Economic Development Administration, that the restoration and adaptation is taking place.

The $1.1-million construction project is divided into three

consecutive phases. The first, currently underway, will focus on audience comfort and amenities. The auditorium floor will be rebuilt to provide proper sight lines, and seating will be reduced from 1,000 to 800. Space for the physically handicapped will be provided. In addition, the acoustical quality of the theater will be upgraded. The entire building, a two-story office development located on the corner of a commercial intersection, will be brought up to current architectural and engineering code specifications. Both interior and exterior spaces will be refurbished, with an eye toward faithful restoration when possible. For instance, the lobby's colorful tiles and elegant hand-painted murals depicting Southwest Indian tribal life will be restored. Outside, the 1950s existing marquee will be removed, and the original decorative terra-cotta corbels and motifs, damaged during the installation of that marquee, restored. Other exterior details will be restored according to original Boller Brothers architectural drawings. The anticipated completion date for the first phase of the project is July 1982.

The second phase of the project will include the rebuilding of the balcony floor to provide adequate sight lines, and installation of new projection booth and sound and light control facilities. Stage expansion also is scheduled. Like many theaters, the KiMo sits surrounded by right-of-ways that constrain through-wall expansion. The architect's alternative is to extend usable stage space toward the auditorium. Although this modification at the KiMo will result in fewer seats,

the end product will be an intimate theater with stage facilities adequate to support diverse programming.

The third and final stage of the KiMo project calls for a rebuilding of the stage and fly loft with complete rigging. The area of the original orchestra pit also will be enlarged. Office spaces at the second and third floors will be remodeled into exhibition space, and new heating and air conditioning equipment will be installed.

The three-phase restoration schedule will allow the theater to begin operation as soon as possible. Because income and promotional leverage generated by the extent of community use will influence the KiMo's future, the phased schedule invites community interest and participation in the restoration effort itself. Inasmuch as Albuquerque now enjoys a rapidly growing affluent population that increasingly demands quality entertainment, the theater's future appears promising.

"Washington has its Kennedy Center... we have the Publick Playhouse"

PUBLICK PLAYHOUSE FOR THE PERFORMING ARTS, CHEVERLY, MARYLAND

When it first opened in 1947, Maryland's Cheverly Theatre, now the Publick Playhouse, was a one-story box, lacking both stage and balcony. The theater was embellished with a stylized Streamline Moderne facade. In 1969, after suffering an

The Streamline 1947 Cheverly Theatre, now the Publick Playhouse for the Performing Arts, in Prince George's County, Maryland, a suburb of Washington, D.C.

irreversible decline in box-office sales, the theater closed. It remained dark (and something of an annoyance to area residents) until the Maryland National Park and Planning Commission purchased it in 1975.

Cheverly is located in Prince George's County, a suburban area of Washington, D.C. Despite its mushrooming population, the county's proliferation of arts groups had until recently little more than school auditoriums, community centers, and churches to satisfy their increasing need for performance space. When the Prince George's Little Theatre took the initiative and petitioned local public officials to provide a permanent public performing arts facility, the county boasted more than 50 choral and instrumental music organizations, 19 theater companies, and four dance groups. Citizen pressure and support for the arts eventually resulted in a Cultural Arts Facilities Study, conducted by the Park and Planning Commission, which affirmed the government's inadequate support for local performing arts events.

Renovation of the Cheverly Theatre began in October 1976. The architects first removed a portion of the rear wall and, in an area located behind the original theater, constructed dressing rooms and other stage services. Seats were then removed in order to install a 30-foot-deep thrust stage with variable wings and proscenium, and stage technology was brought up-to-date. The former projection booth was transformed into a production control room equipped with a 36-channel, 21-scene preset dimmer board. A complete sound system with clear intercom service connecting the control booth with backstage and dressing room areas also was installed. The theater maintains a small inventory of theatrical soft goods, including scrims, travelers, and curtains, and from time to time employs a movable dance floor, black or white, which fits precisely over the stage surface.

Friends of the Publick Playhouse, Inc., a nonprofit citizen support group, was established in 1976 "to provide services and seek donations which will benefit the community artists as users of the theatre." Since then, the friends have netted landscaping, a piano, auditorium carpeting, marquee lettering, and the graphic design for the theater facade. Using fundraising proceeds, the organization has contributed lighting instruments, audio equipment, and choral risers to the facility.

Owned and operated by the Maryland National Capital Park and Planning Commission, the revitalized 462-seat Publick Playhouse has functioned successfully with a year-round calendar since its reopening in October 1976. (The Playhouse staff of 10 includes managing and technical directors, clerical assistants, technicians, and custodians.) The theater's multi-purpose stage has played host to more than 500 performances by community and professional theater, dance, and music groups. The facility is also used for educational programs, workshops, and symposia patronized by all age groups and representing a broad spectrum of interests. As one local newspaper critic asserted, "Washington may have its Kennedy Center, but we have the Publick Playhouse."

Moorish details of Atlanta's monumental 1929 Fox Theatre. The bands of colored brick, seen here on a minaret, are a Fox signature.

Atlanta rallies to save the landmark Fox

FOX THEATRE, ATLANTA, GEORGIA

Only three movie palaces have been designated National Historic Landmarks: the Ohio, in Columbus; the Paramount, in Oakland; and the Fox, in Atlanta. Each is an elaborate downtown showcase once threatened with the specter of demolition, but saved by local citizens determined to protect their community's heritage. In the case of the 1929 Fox, a giant fortress-like structure, 1974 was the year of judgment. The theater was dark, and Southern Bell Telephone and Telegraph stood ready to exercise its option on the property and erect a major new office complex in place of the palace's exotic minarets.

In order to consolidate efforts to save the theater, community activists founded Atlanta Landmarks, a nonprofit organization, to work for the protection of the Fox as well as other historic local structures. Atlanta Landmarks marshaled adequate public support (about 2,500 citizens attended a public rally on behalf of the Fox) to generate an $11,000 feasibility study on the theater paid for with state historic preservation funds.

Buying the time to develop alternatives for use of the theater was nearly as important as finding the funds to implement those alternatives. Encouraged by a promising evaluation of the theater's economic potential, the city of Atlanta withheld Southern Bell's demolition permit for eight months. This moratorium gave Atlanta Landmarks time to negotiate a $1.8-million loan from a consortium of five local banks. Eventually, Southern Bell, a cooperative player from the start, agreed to turn over to Landmarks the option to purchase the Fox parcel at a cost of $1.8 million (the value of the land alone). Southern Bell then acquired the balance of the block of land on which the Fox is located and recently erected an office tower for its requisite spatial expansion.

Soon after acquiring the Fox, Atlanta Landmarks began restoration of the theater. A long list of much needed improvements and repairs began with the replacement of the theater's roof. With the help of a $200,000 grant from the U.S. Department of Housing and Urban Development, the original design of the theater's facade, together with nine ground-level storefronts, was fully restored. Within the theater's entrance arcade, the use of multiple glazes, stencils, and gilding restored the original brilliance of the Moorish decor. In the auditorium itself, the enormous atmospheric ceiling was repainted to provide a screen for the Fox cloud machine and the restored sunrise and sunset lighting effects. Stageside of the proscenium arch, major improvements in production technology are complete. Three exotic ballrooms within the Fox building have been restored to the degree that they can be used frequently, and full-scale restoration will be carried out as funds become available.

The Fox has benefited from numerous substantial financial contributions, ranging from $5,000 to $440,000, from individual donors. A $.25-per-ticket surcharge, instituted shortly after Atlanta Landmarks' acquisition of the Fox, continually refreshes renovation funds. The fact that theater-based fundraising events could be held soon after Landmarks' purchase of the Fox influenced the outcome of the building's struggle for survival. Had Landmarks defaulted on either the loan interest or principal payments, its option to purchase the Fox would have been forfeited, and the theater lost. However, the movie palace's demonstrated earning power attracted corporate as well as state and federal government contributions, and a development campaign generated the remainder of the funds necessary for Landmarks to hold title to the Fox. The theater's earning power is still readily apparent, and a $250,000 operating profit in its first three years of use has been reinvested to preserve and restore its grandeur on a continuing basis.

SPECIAL PURPOSE PERFORMING ARTS CENTERS

Particularly in larger cities, where competition for performing dates can be fierce, multiple-purpose theaters do not necessarily meet the special needs of arts organizations dedicated to one art form. In St. Louis, Providence, and other cities, symphony orchestras and repertory theater groups have discovered the advantages of adaptive use for their individual purposes. The following profiles illustrate the flexibility of movie palaces. In light of their extensive technical, acoustical, and spatial rearrangements, recycled theaters have proved to be remarkably resilient.

Magnificent acoustics in a changing neighborhood

POWELL SYMPHONY HALL, ST. LOUIS, MISSOURI

New York Times architecture critic Ada Louise Huxtable called it "one of the more significant pieces of fallout of the cultural explosion" of the late 1960s. (42) Violinist Isaac Stern assessed it as "one of the three great concert halls in America." All things considered, Powell Symphony Hall is an important adaptive use achievement, its conversion from St. Louis Theatre less a matter of preservation than a brave experiment in acoustical engineering and theater design. When it opened in 1968, Powell's conversion from movie palace to concert hall was the first such transformation in the United States.

The financing of Powell Hall, a 1926 Rapp and Rapp design, began in 1965 with a conditional $500,000 gift from a prominent St. Louis citizen and former Symphony Society president, Oscar Johnson, Jr. His endowment carried with it the

Architect's longitudinal section of Powell Symphony Hall, using French baroque spatial devices.

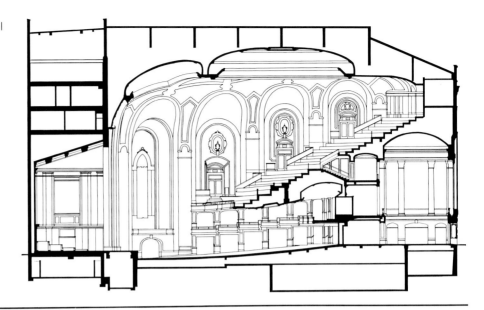

Powell Hall's elegant grand stair. (left).

stipulation that before December 1966, the full sum had to be applied to the acquisition of a permanent home for the 87-year-old St. Louis Symphony. The society's search for a new hall led to the consideration of numerous alternatives, but when the owner of the St. Louis Theatre decided to leave the neighborhood, remodeling and renovation of the theater became the most attractive and least costly option. The Symphony had performed in the St. Louis Theatre several years earlier and discovered that its auditorium acoustics were well above average. After acoustical experts and architects had thoroughly tested the St. Louis, the Symphony purchased the theater as its new home.

To meet the estimated $2-million restoration costs, the St. Louis Symphony launched a capital fundraising campaign. The first campaign goal was to match a $2-million Ford Foundation grant, and the development fund was considerably fortified by a $1-million trust given by the widow of Walter S. Powell, in whose honor the hall was subsequently named. St. Louis patrons contributed generously to support the facility, and by the time the hall opened, the fund's reserves totaled $4 million, $13,000 in excess of the Symphony's goal.

RENOVATION FOR SUPERIOR ACOUSTICS

From the beginning, the renovation effort was directed toward the creation of a superior acoustical environment for the country's second oldest orchestra. The Symphony retained

Dr. Cyril M. Harris, professor of engineering and architecture at Columbia University and acoustical consultant for such halls as New York's Metropolitan Opera House. Dr. Harris' four principal design challenges of the project were to reduce the volume of the hall; increase the diffusion of sound; design a backstage enclosure as part of the auditorium; and select interior finishes and furnishings.

New sidewalls of uniform thickness were designed and constructed to seal undesirable sound traps and reduce the volume of the auditorium. The rear walls of the orchestra, grand tier, and balcony were moved forward and redesigned to support overall acoustical dynamics. The stage area was rebuilt to accommodate the installation of a classically designed orchestra shell constructed behind an enlarged proscenium opening, which served to integrate the stage and auditorium. A new stage floor was constructed, and special removable wood risers were built for the musicians. The orchestra also received entirely new oak flooring constructed above the original concrete surface. Unnecessary auditorium openings were sealed and fitted with convex cylindrical surfaces offset within existing columns to provide optimal diffusion of sound. All furnishings and mechanical systems in the hall were evaluated and treated in relationship to desired acoustical quality.

Other areas of the theater which were redesigned include the grand foyer and service facilities. A white, crimson,

and gold (24-carat gold leaf, which at the time exhausted all available U.S. supplies) interior theme enhanced new Louis XV chandeliers and other accessories assembled to capture the desired 18th-century French baroque style. The theater's mezzanine was transformed into grand tier boxes with private anterooms.

Three floors of administrative office space were constructed within the existing stage house above the 35-foot-high orchestra shell. The projection booth became a small recording studio. Lighting systems, storage facilities, dressing rooms, and other service areas were all designed with state-of-the-art thoroughness, including humidity control for instruments and an intercom system connecting stage activity with dressing rooms and offices.

INTERNATIONALLY RANKED FACILITY

Today, after nearly 14 years of 52-week seasons, Powell Symphony Hall has an international ranking as a concert facility with exceptional acoustics. In 1966, at the time the decision was made to establish a permanent home for the Symphony, the cost of a new hall was estimated at between $15 million and $20 million. The Symphony purchased and renovated the St. Louis Theatre for well under $3 million, a significant fiscal accomplishment.

Ongoing issues faced by the Symphony include limited parking facilities and a tenuous neighborhood context, but neither has seriously influenced attendance figures. In fact, the area is beginning to exhibit signs of moderate redevelopment, and the future augurs slow but steady revitalization owing in part to the renaissance of the old St. Louis Theatre.

"Beg! Borrow before you buy!"

COMMUNITY THEATRE, CEDAR RAPIDS, IOWA

It would be difficult to improve on this in-house description of how the Community Theatre in Cedar Rapids, Iowa, located a permanent performing space:

In 1954, while scouring the city for possible land sites, the director of Cedar Rapids' Community Theatre (then the Footlighters Theater) wandered into a dilapidated movie theatre on Third Street SE called the "Strand." Sitting down and watching a "D" movie, he began to wonder if by many stretches of the imagination, the Community Theatre had found a home. This theatre had been built in 1912 and had seen everything from *The Perils of Pauline* to westerns and Czech films, with the doors closing permanently in 1954. It was no snap decision to buy the old theatre. A steady parade of contractors, engineers, electricians, architects, and plumbers combed the building. Planning meetings were held, a fund drive organized and scores of volunteers recruited. For weeks, it was "wreck, wrack and ruin"—all in 100-degree heat. The motto was "Beg! Borrow before you buy!" But the task was accomplished and the reborn theatre opened its doors in October, 1955, with the

Architect's original rendering for the 1917 Majestic Theatre in Providence (left), and the Majestic today, the home of Trinity Square Repertory Company (right).

production of *Happy Birthday*. Aided by the sale of some property, the Strand cost some $30,000 with an additional $9,200 in donated services. Five hundred fifteen angels helped and the mortgage was paid off in two years. This theatre stands as a "testimonial to the generous and cooperative spirit of a community." (43)

Ironically, the Community Theatre has outgrown its 1954 home. Although the house is still used as the company's headquarters and for smaller productions, the Community Theatre is now staging major productions in Cedar Rapids' recently renovated movie palace, the Paramount Theatre for the Performing Arts, a 1920s Rapp and Rapp structure purchased by the city in 1976.

Trinity Rep finds a fitting home

LEDERER THEATRE, PROVIDENCE, RHODE ISLAND

Like Macon's Grand Opera House, the Lederer Theatre in Providence, Rhode Island, represents a slice of 20th-century American show business history. When the Lederer, now the home of Trinity Square Repertory Company, first opened in 1917 as the Majestic, the William Walker and Son design brought this seacoast town a lavish Italianate palace embellished with a terra-cotta and colored glass canopy for each of its five entrances. Within less than a year, the owners entered into a

lease agreement with the Shubert organization, which brought Providence patrons entertainment ranging from legitimate drama to musical revues.

The resident acting company that occupied the theater during its last two years as a legitimate house was swept off its stage by the tide rising from Hollywood. In 1923 the Majestic's owners decided against renewing the lease agreement with Shubert, opting instead for silent film. Under new ownership, the Majestic bought exclusive territorial rights to the revolutionary Warner Vitaphone in 1926, and in so doing screened the first motion pictures to talk to Providence.

DECLINE AND ASCENT

As the Majestic entered the era of its decline, the Trinity Square Repertory Company, under the direction of founding artistic director Adrian Hall, embarked on its remarkable ascent. In 1964, with the support of a few enthusiastic citizens, the professional acting group set up residence in a Sunday School building attached to the Trinity Square United Methodist Church. After two years a series of national grants allowed the company to expand its production capability, and the troupe performed for the next nine seasons both at the original 300-seat theater and in a larger 1,000-seat auditorium rented from and shared with the Rhode Island School of Design (RISD). Early experience with "found" theater space was less an obstacle than a laboratory to Adrian Hall, and as he adapted the two theaters to accommodate an increasingly experimental repertoire, the spatial relationship between audience and actor emerged as a distinguishing element in the company's artistic philosophy. Worldwide recognition, a bevy of awards, and a series of appearances on national public television brought the Trinity Rep to the forefront of American theater.

In 1970 the Foundation for Repertory Theatre of Rhode Island, which had acted as the community support group for Trinity Rep since the company's inception, purchased the Majestic Theater for $175,000. The relatively small sum reflects a financial contribution on the part of the former owners. The Majestic was subsequently renamed the Lederer in honor of a major contributor whose incremental gift became the basis for a five-year foundation fundraising campaign.

DESIGN FOR ARTISTIC PHILOSOPHY
New design alternatives for the old vaudeville house were explored in relationship to the artistic philosophy of Trinity Rep. Working closely with the renovation architects, Adrian Hall and resident designer Eugene Lee tailored the design of a completely reconstructed facility to the concepts around which the theater company had evolved. The original auditorium, lower balcony, and proscenium were dismantled and removed. Subsequently, a poured-in-place concrete floor was installed from the level of the lower balcony to the

original stage area, creating two distinct performing spaces, one over the other. An intimate, 297-seat theater with an adjustable three-quarter round stage space (projecting from the backstage toward the audience) was constructed. Above, the space was designed as essentially a large empty box in which seating and stage could be rearranged to suit the requirements of each new production. The maximum capacity in the upper theater, originally 800, was reduced in 1978 to accommodate studio/classroom space for the Rep's professional acting conservatory.

Throughout the two-year construction period, the Rep continued to perform at its two "found" theaters, and in 1973 moved to the completed Lederer. Today, the Foundation for Repertory Theater owns and meets mortgage payments on the Lederer complex, which includes the two theaters, scene and costume shops, rehearsal hall, box offices, graphics department, and administrative office space. The foundation leases the Lederer at a cost of one dollar per year to the Trinity Personna Company, a nonprofit corporation established by community leaders and theater personnel to manage the day-to-day operation of the facility.

In 1972 the old Majestic Theatre, with a restored exterior and lobby space, was entered on the National Register of Historic Places with the following statement of significance:

Although it is about to embark on a new life—housing new, alive performers using innovative and lively forms of dramatic

expression, the Majestic Theatre Building will remain a prominent physical reminder of the era of the extravagant and luxurious "movie palaces" constructed in America during the second-through-fourth decades of the century. (44)

PRIVATE DEVELOPMENT INVESTMENT

With increasing frequency, the private sector is reaping the profit potential of restored movie palaces. From road show programming to mixed entertainment calendars, the following projects demonstrate how the sensitive restoration of older theaters can be by itself an effective promotional tool, not to mention a public-spirited investment.

Spain in Santa Barbara

ARLINGTON CENTER FOR THE PERFORMING ARTS,
SANTA BARBARA, CALIFORNIA

Santa Barbara is located 80 miles from downtown Los Angeles on an elysian coastal plain between the Santa Ynez mountains and the Pacific Ocean. Architect Charles Moore described the city as "an architectural idiom of white stucco walls, big leafed plants, bougainvillea, low pitched Mediterranean tile roofs, and gentle silhouettes against a deep blue sky." (45)

In this spirit, the Fox Arlington Theatre was constructed in 1931 as an affectionate gesture to Santa Barbara, much of which had been shattered by a 1925 earthquake. The 1,800-seat theater was in fact named after the Arlington Hotel, a casualty of the earthquake and former occupant of the Fox Arlington site. Architects Edwards, Plunkett, and Howells conceived of the project as a small Spanish mission village and created a sequence of ever-increasing scale culminating in a "cathedral," its six-story campanile supporting the revolving Fox neon sign. Small stucco retail shops, each a variation on the central theme, were placed in front of the larger structure. Just behind the row of shops, open-air porch-like lobbies, landscaped courtyards and patios, arcades, and tiled fountains contribute to the overall Andalusian mystique.

The entry sequence is entirely out-of-doors under the cover of the open loggia, its center featuring a narrow fountain finished in colorful patterns of Spanish tilework. *A Progressive Architecture* article describes the approach:

The Arlington is entered through a series of spatial progressions which, in the best Baroque tradition, commence the experience of theater well before the actual performance begins. One first proceeds through two arcades, white stucco bounded by squat pink columns....and arched colonnades overlooking growths of

The Arlington's interior courtyards and loggia (above) help to convey an impression of rural Spain. Adjacent shopfronts are integrated into the design of the 1931 Spanish Revival movie palace, now the Arlington Center for the Performing Arts in Santa Barbara (right).

sub-tropical foliage. Sturdy overhead beams are picked out with delicate pastel florets, and above the door to the theater's interior, a mural depicts coy senoritas and dashing caballeros abandoning themselves to the strains of an unheard flamenco....(46)

Inside the theater, the stucco facades of the auditorium side-walls are graced by gables and sheds, the roof forms of rural Spain. Wrought iron details, balconies, porches, chimneys, lanterns, and thick, arched doorways express the romantic continuity between city and theater.

MODEST REHABILITATION INSPIRES
MAJOR REVITALIZATION

After acquiring the Fox Arlington in 1976, the Los Angeles-based Metropolitan Theatres Corporation inaugurated a modest program of repainting and recarpeting. The project escalated to include major interior rehabilitation, upgrading of stage facilities, seating capacity increased to over 2,000, and acoustical improvements. The first phase of what is now intended as an ongoing restoration effort was completed at a cost estimated between $700,000 and $800,000, or about $400 per seat.

The original building, designed to resist earthquake loads, combined rigid steel framing with concrete infill panels and reinforced concrete construction. The structure was found to be sound. Mechanical and electrical service was brought up to operational standards, although improvements are still planned for both systems. Work proceeded with the comprehensive repainting of interior and exterior surfaces, which included the replacement of missing decorative elements, restoration of interior woodwork and original seating, and installation of new carpeting.

The theater stage and service spaces were redesigned to accommodate contemporary performing arts. The fly loft received completely new rigging, the orchestra pit greater area and depth. Stage lighting controlled from the original light board was restored to full operation and augmented with a new dimming system. Backstage, underutilized areas were redesigned to create additional service space. Reclaimed square footage was applied to the design of restroom facilities, and a green room for performers and all existing dressing rooms were completely refurbished. Shallow wings and lack of stage crossover space remain present-day liabilities.

ARTS FOR PROFIT

Not long after the start of the restoration campaign, the Arlington Center for the Performing Arts opened its doors. Its reprogramming package represents an unusual cooperation between private enterprise and community service. The theater is now the home of the Santa Barbara Symphony and the Community Arts Music Association. From June 15 to September 15 the Metropolitan books first-run motion pic-

A familiar face in downtown Baraboo, Wisconsin: the Al Ringling Theatre (far left) and an early photograph of the 1915 Al Ringling auditorium (left), a miniaturization of the opera house at Versailles. (right) A frieze detail in the Al Ringling lobby.

tures to capitalize on Santa Barbara's summer audience. For the duration of the fiscal year, the theater switches to its performing arts calendar, in part managed by the Symphony and the Community Arts Music Association.

As a result of this split-season programming, the city enjoys more than 100 performances annually. The schedule features eight to 20 performances by the Santa Barbara Symphony and six to eight performances by visiting orchestras—in recent years, the Minneapolis, Tokyo, Philadelphia, and Cleveland. The Arlington's original marquee has also recently announced ballet and opera productions. In addition to these presentations, the center is used by local colleges and universities for several subscription series. Touring road shows, Las Vegas stage acts, and rock and jazz concerts all take place under the Arlington's atmospheric sky with its blinking stars.

The arts-for-profit formula is working well in Santa Barbara. Plans for the second major phase of Arlington restoration, including installation of a new mechanical plant and additional new acoustical treatments, now are under consideration. The Arlington Center for the Performing Arts began with an uncommon movie palace in an uncommon city, the two joined by shared heritage and mutual regard for historical continuity. It is therefore not surprising that the transformation of the Fox Arlington involved an atypical investment by a private theater chain working with the cooperation and full support of the local community. In a sense, Charles Moore

captured the significance of their relationship in his celebration of Santa Barbara's urban imagination: ". . . . by encouraging and dramatizing the act of public habitation, the city builders have made a stage for daily action and encounter as rich as any devised in Hollywood." (47)

A theater and a town: loyal to each other

AL RINGLING THEATRE, BARABOO, WISCONSIN

The Al Ringling Theatre has survived its first 66 years insulated from the economic decline suffered by nearly all of its larger urban counterparts. It appears today much the way it did in 1915, a respectful miniaturization of the 18th-century opera house at Versailles. The design of the 804-seat theater helped to launch the careers of C. W. and George L. Rapp, the nation's most prolific and influential movie palace architects. The building, designed as a vaudeville/movie house, remains a vital fixture in downtown Baraboo, Wisconsin, adapting to changing times. It continues to operate as it has for the better part of the century, earning its own way as a movie house and multi-purpose theater.

The endurance of the Al Ringling is not a matter of chance. The theater was commissioned by and named after the eldest of the famous Ringling brothers, who intended to give it to

the community of Baraboo. (48) After his death in 1916, the four brothers purchased the building from his widow. The theater was held in the Ringling family for the next 37 years, a significant factor in the maintenance of its original design. The few necessary modifications required by improved exhibition technology and other functional adjustments were closely governed by family interests. The sale of the Al Ringling in 1953 stipulated the restriction of any significant alterations. (49) In this manner, the theater escaped the fate of most chain-operated or corporately owned movie palaces, slipping past the Depression years protected by memorial significance and the Ringling family's ownership.

PRESERVATION THROUGH PROGRAMMING

Baraboo has not outgrown the Al Ringling. The values of its first owners, although steeped in showmanship, were tied to the quality of entertainment desired by local patrons. The ongoing balance between sensitive programming and community expectations has led to the natural "preservation" not only of the historically significant theater, but also of the community institution it has grown to represent. Performing arts events are scheduled four to five times per year, and although artists from across the country perform at the theater, rental rates are reasonable ($200 to $500 depending on the day of the week), encouraging bookings by local groups. Nonprofit groups are eligible for reduced rates, and all groups provide

their own box-office and custodial staff. (50) Children's matinees and family entertainment continue to stimulate downtown activity. More to the point, the theater operates 364 days a year, closing only for Christmas.

RESTORATION AS A LOCAL ACT OF LOYALTY

The current owner of the Al Ringling has recently undertaken careful restoration of interior decor. The organ has been fully restored, as has about 95 percent of the seating. In keeping with the spirit of the town's miniature movie palace, high school volunteers are assisting in the theater restoration efforts. In addition, some structural repairs have been undertaken.

Remarkably, although all new lines are used on stage, the fly loft and most of the rigging have served the community's needs adequately, and eight of the original 11 dressing rooms are in good repair. The original fire curtain and two hand-painted stock settings from the 1920s also remain in remarkable condition.

The role of a theater (qualified by size and stability) in the life of the town defines a fundamental principle that connects the arts to the community and the community to local business. What could be more optimal than a tidy but appropriately ornate multiple-use performing arts facility located roughly in the middle of the central business district? In the case of Baraboo, the theater stands directly across from the

Unique fan-vaulted ceiling in San Francisco's restored Golden Gate Theatre. Cables had ripped through the vaulting in the 1960s when a drop ceiling was installed to form a second viewing room.

sedate Sauk County Courthouse, just inside the southwest corner of the Baraboo town square, where the Al Ringling will no doubt remain for the enjoyment of future generations.

Profit-making reuse above the Pacific

GOLDEN GATE THEATRE, SAN FRANCISCO, CALIFORNIA

The Golden Gate in San Francisco is one of three theaters in the Bay City owned and operated by James L. Nederlander and Carole J. Shorenstein. The Nederlander organization, a Broadway-based entertainment organization, also owns and operates houses in Detroit, Chicago, New York, Los Angeles, and other major cities in the United States. Nederlander's 1979 restoration of the theater brought full cycle a history that reflects the machinations of Hollywood's early years.

Commissioned by the Orpheum circuit in 1922, the Golden Gate was the twenty-first of more than 50 theaters designed by G. Albert Landsburgh, a noted San Francisco architect. Constructed as part of an eight-story office building complex, the 2,800-seat theater featured an unusual corner marquee, elaborate fan vaulting in the grand lobby, and a stylized French rococo auditorium. In its heyday, the Golden Gate boasted a large stage, library for the orchestra's musicians, rehearsal area, nursery, animal room, in-house valet/tailor, lavish dressing rooms, and other amenities. Live stage presentations continued by popular demand until the unusually late

year of 1954. After that time, first-run movies were the featured programs.

When the Golden Gate finally closed in 1972, its original grandeur lay hidden under years of "modernization" and neglect. The theater's bisection into "piggyback" cinemas and the installation of an escalator to service the second-level screen, adapted from the existing balcony, introduced the most difficult restoration challenge. The disassembly and removal of the 118-by-18-foot steel truss implanted to support the "floor" of the twin cinema involved 14 tons of excess steel, plaster, sheetrock, studs, and insulation. The escalator was removed to restore the original marble stair, and the original balcony sight lines were reconstructed. Painstaking restoration eventually returned the Golden Gate to its early elegance, and the theater reopened to public kudos on December 27, 1979. Its first season included *A Chorus Line*, *The Music Man*, *The Best Little Whorehouse in Texas*, *Camelot*, and *My Fair Lady*, a preview of the Golden Gate's successful new Broadway touring programming.

The Nederlander organization currently operates several houses constructed during the 1920s and, like the Golden Gate, restored and utilized as first-rate road show facilities. The availability of movie palaces and vaudeville theaters, such as Nederlander's Fisher in Detroit and Mark Hellinger in New York, has helped private enterprise to capitalize on the growing public demand for live quality theatrical entertainment. The public, of course, also benefits, for regardless of theater

The 1926 Warner Theatre today in downtown Washington, D.C. The Warner is typical of movie palaces developed in conjunction with office buildings.

ownership—private or public—the renaissance of movie palaces brings a new vitality to urban districts and the larger surrounding community. (51)

Bicentennial, rock, and Broadway: combination for success

WARNER THEATRE, WASHINGTON, D.C.

The performing arts have enjoyed burgeoning good health in the nation's capital during the past decade, and a growing professional population coupled with the steady growth of the downtown residential real estate market continues to whet the demand for evening cultural events. It is not surprising, then, that the Warner Theatre, one of the few remaining movie palaces in Washington's central business district, has established itself among the city's better stages.

The Warner, located three blocks east of the White House, opened in 1927 as the Earle. The theater was the keystone of a 10-story, 200-unit office complex that included a large basement restaurant and 1,500-seat roof garden. C. Howard Crane and Kenneth Franzheim, the well-known Detroit-based movie palace architects retained to design the theater, delivered an elegant mix of Louis XIV and late Empire, featuring a long, heavily mirrored, three-story entrance lobby. Ozark marble and custom-designed tapestries enriched its original green and gold decor. (52)

The Earle billed itself as "America's perfect theatre" and prospered with vaudeville/motion picture programming. Eddie Cantor, Sophie Tucker, George Jessel, and Ethel Barrymore were among the many great names to perform before Earle audiences. In 1926, Harry Warner's Warner Bros. took control of the theater from the Crandell circuit. Coasting through the Depression, the Earle became Warner Bros.' Washington showcase for new film releases premiered with stage shows featuring such stars as Glenn Miller and Martha Raye. The day after World War II ended, in response to the growing popularity and abundance of "major motion pictures," the theater ended its tradition of shows. Warner changed the name of the theater in 1947, and it remained a first-run house until the 1968 riots set much of the surrounding business district aflame. In 1971 the theater screened its last film.

Bicentennial enthusiasm helped bring the Warner neighborhood back to life. The area has become one of ongoing concerted reinvestment: several multimillion-dollar mixed-use development projects are under construction, restoration programs are approaching completion, and the adjacent Pennsylvania Avenue redevelopment effort will substantially upgrade the district's southern edge. In the middle of this restoration and redevelopment activity sits the rejuvenated Warner, fortuitously less than two blocks from Metro Center, heart of the city's new mass transit system.

Reuse of the theater began in 1977 when the office building's new owners leased the facility to Cellar Door Produc-

Early photographs of the 1927 Oriental Theatre in Milwaukee, with its onion-domed minarets (left) and grand lobby (right). Note the elephant head column capitals and lions guarding the stairway.

tions, the metropolitan area's largest rock concert promoter. In October of that year, Cellar Door began a $100,000 year-long refurbishment of the Warner. Not long after Cellar Door completed its upgrading of the facility, the organization amicably parted ways with the theater so that the current Warner operation could pursue a diversified entertainment format. To date, approximately $250,000 has been funneled into renovation and technical improvements, a figure that will likely grow with the management's plan for incremental restoration. The 2,000-person capacity auditorium has been reseated, lighting has been modernized, and the dressing rooms have been refurbished. Eventually, the Warner management hopes to repair the proscenium arch, which was partially defaced in the theater's 1953 conversion to Cinerama.

The programming concept that determines the Warner's calendar reflects Washington's diverse population. Because of stage limitations—its vaudeville-sized dimensions are constrained by inalterable right-of-ways—the theater can accommodate neither large musical productions nor grand opera. Nearly all other art forms, however, can be accommodated. Broadway shows that have booked the Warner include *For Colored Girls Who Have Considered Suicide/When the Rainbow is Enuf*, *Chapter Two*, *Your Arms Too Short to Box with God*, *Fiddler on the Roof*, and *Othello*.

In addition to touring productions, the Warner hosts events produced by the Washington Performing Arts Society, including children's opera and performances by African and Latin American dance groups. Concert dates remain in the Warner calendar, punctuating the longer-running stage productions with rock, pop, new wave, and jazz music. The management also books local, community-based events, and special presentations such as Israel's Puppet Theatre, the Miss Black America D.C. Pageant, and video coverage of international soccer championships have utilized the theater's facilities.

The Warner Theatre, a private sector enterprise, augments income from ticket sales, theater rentals, and concessions with in-house production efforts. It comfortably shares the Washington performing arts market with the Kennedy Center's Eisenhower Theater and the historic National Theater, located just a half block away. The press and general public have readily welcomed the Warner to a growing cultural environment richer for its revitalization.

A chain of successes

ORIENTAL LANDMARK THEATRE, MILWAUKEE, WISCONSIN

Like Baraboo's Al Ringling, Milwaukee's Oriental Theatre still serves its original purpose. Although regularly scheduled live entertainment and first-run films faded from its marquee long ago, the local landmark benefits from a natural rhythm of repair that has preserved its opening day ambience without the help of an expensive restoration campaign. The theater has been continuously supported by steady patron-

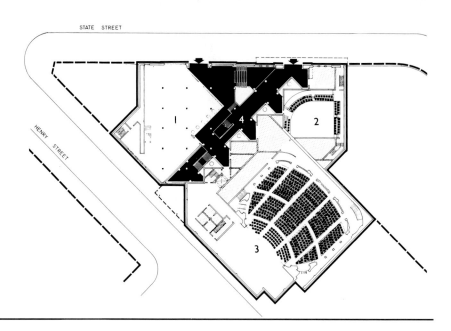

Architect's drawing of the Madison Civic Center's State Street level. Legend: 1, Madison Art Center; 2, Isthmus Playhouse; 3, Oscar Mayer Theatre; 4, Crossroads.

age, in no small part the product of a creative repertory film program brought to Milwaukee by the Oriental's current management, Landmark Theatre Corporation of Los Angeles.

A devotion to film, an eye for older theaters, and a business insight into an underdeveloped entertainment market led to the founding of Parallax Theatre Corporation (renamed Landmark in 1980). Since its inception less than 10 years ago, Landmark's chain has grown to include 29 screens in 15 states. The Landmark distribution concept is based on a lower-priced, double-feature classic and genre film calendar that changes bills daily. More than 60 different films are offered monthly to a target audience of well-educated 18- to 35-year-olds.

Landmark's Oriental, built by Milwaukee architects Dick and Bauer in 1927 at a cost of $1.7 million, seats about 2,000 patrons. Its facade sports two towers, each capped by highly visible onion domes. The theater is the flagship for a half-block, two-story retail/office/entertainment complex with five storefronts, a bar and bowling alley in the basement, and a corner drugstore. Typical of the late 1920s first-run movie palaces, the Oriental sits on a major thoroughfare (over the intersection of two trolley lines) that is now midway between a 22,000-student university campus and the center of downtown Milwaukee.

The theater's decor is, as its name suggests, culled from Near Eastern images. The balcony stair is flanked by seated lions, and deep beams spanning the two-story grand lobby are supported by elephant-head capitals. In the auditorium between pilasters sit Buddhas, their electric eyes and bejeweled foreheads glowing throughout performances. Although the theater is beginning to show its middle age, it is respected by its patrons and management and remains an important East Side Milwaukee landmark and neighborhood movie palace.

As theater owners begin to feel the pressure of home video and cable television, Landmark is capitalizing on the "theatergoing experience." In addition to the Oriental, the chain operates the Uptown in Minneapolis, Varsity in Evanston, UC Theatre in Berkeley, Rialto in South Pasadena, and Ogden in Denver. All are late 1920s or early '30s theaters, and their rescue by Landmark augurs well for the rescue of other such gems by theater owners across the country.

MUNICIPAL REDEVELOPMENT ANCHOR

The relationship between performing arts activity and downtown commercial revitalization has added a new dimension to the often unsuccessful urban renewal formulas of the early 1960s. Many cities, in partnership with nonprofit redevelop-

The Madison Civic Center in Madison, Wisconsin, is a reactivated movie palace.

ment corporations and private business, are committed to planning programs that recognize the power of lively cultural facilities to stimulate activity in central business districts. In such cities the arts are helping to illuminate the hours after 5 pm—when most downtowns go dark—and in turn generate demand for ancillary services and jobs. The following portraits reflect the potential of the concept.

State Street becomes a great street

MADISON CIVIC CENTER, MADISON, WISCONSIN

In Madison, Wisconsin, a 1928 movie palace and three adjacent retail properties have been integrated to create a new multi-use civic center in the heart of the capital city's downtown retail neighborhood. The buildings—Rapp and Rapp's Capitol Theatre, a sewing center, fur shop, and department store—have been transformed into a sparkling cultural resource for the visual, performing, and communications arts. The 110,000-square-foot facility features a 2,215-seat auditorium (that of the old Capitol), an intimate 370-seat thrust theater, and an arts center connected by a six-level lobby its architects call "the crossroads."

In 1974, when Madison's mayor led the city drive to purchase the old Capitol Theatre on State Street (and the stores flanking it), he ended a lengthy and colorful debate about the location and design of the city's long-overdue civic

center complex. The Civic Center, located on the city's new State Street transit mall for pedestrians and buses, is only a few blocks from the State Capitol and the University of Wisconsin-Madison campus.

Architects Hardy Holzman Pfeiffer Associates reinterpreted the old movie palace in a completely upgraded auditorium. The existing theater was augmented with new construction and services, and although the 1928 lobby disappeared into the new multistoried lobby, stencils and carefully blended color capture the spirit of the original theater. In the lower level of the lobby, wide stairs have been designed to act as informal bleacher-style seating to utilize the maximum space potential. Sound and light locks allow simultaneous programming and secure each performance space against disturbances.

The proportion of new construction to restored and recycled space is nearly equal. The architects retained the original facade of the theater in a design integrating the symmetrical construction of new walls on either side of the Capitol's Moorish tower. By penetrating a triangular block, service and entry access to the complex were provided on a street located southeast of the main entrance.

CHECKLIST OF CHANGES

In an article published in *Architectural Record*, Hardy Holzman Pfeiffer enumerated by checklist many of the changes made in the transformation from Capitol to Oscar Mayer Theatre. (53) Beginning with the stage, the architects removed the rear

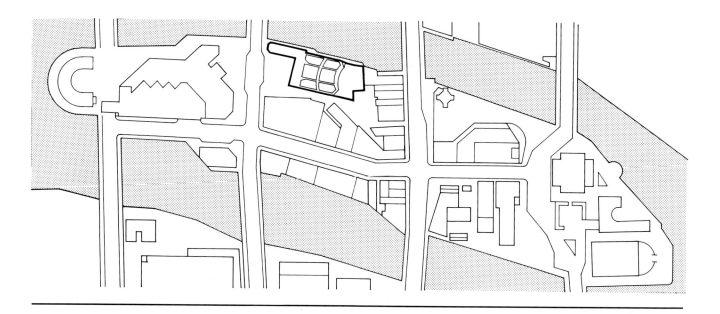

stage wall and added 11 feet to its depth. The design team assembled a state-of-the-art stage package to meet the facility's technical requirements. The new stage lighting system features a memory control console with patch panel and dimmer operating equipment. Acoustical modifications combined an electronic sound system with natural stage-born amplification, controlled and enhanced by a lightweight acoustical shell and special curtain that transmits stage tower volume. The facility's mechanical package was designed to utilize maximum energy efficiency.

The theater's old orchestra pit was replaced with a larger, 56-by-20-foot hydraulically operated platform programmed to stop at four different positions: one level serves loading requirements, another musicians, the third creates space for extra rows of seating, and the fourth extends usable stage area. Star dressing rooms, scenery preparation, and backstage circulation were amply accommodated in the construction of 1,900 additional square feet of stage left wing space. Two new chorus dressing rooms were located beneath the stage area. New construction also created 1,900 square feet of administrative space and a 1,900-square-foot rehearsal room.

Funding of the Madison Civic Center goes back to 1954, when the city floated $5 million in civic center bonds, repaid in 1974. In July 1977, the city raised $2 million in 10-year promissory notes for the project. The year following, another $1.6 million was raised by the Greater Madison Foundation for the Arts, Inc., from private sector resources. In 1979 the city received $760,000 ($400,000 in federal funds) in direct appropriation within the provisions of the general revenue-sharing program. The remaining funds were generated through the sale of additional city promissory notes.

The revenue-sharing funds were spent on complementary programs, including two rehearsal rooms, a closed-circuit television system, and other equipment. In 1981, $255,000 in capital improvement funds helped to finance a banquet room, cable TV studio for community video programming, and stage workshop area.

A STATEWIDE RESOURCE

The Madison Civic Center is a statewide resource. Its programming, which includes activities by such groups as the Children's Theater, Madison Civic Repertory, Wisconsin Chamber Orchestra, Madison Civic Music Association, and Madison Symphony, hints at the total potential of the center's annual 52-week operation. Strong city management involvement is committed to promoting and co-promoting an expanded range of cultural events representing the diverse heritage of the state. The civic center's reduced rental rates for nonprofit groups are designed to encourage broad programming.

After one year of operation, the civic center has already had a visible impact on the life of the city and its downtown retail district. Thus Madison joins a growing list of mid-sized

Aerial plan of Stolp Island, Aurora, showing location of the Paramount Arts Centre.

View along Stolp Island toward the Aurora Paramount.

cities that have recognized and acted upon the cultural and economic advantages of linking performing arts activities and the central business district. Significantly, Madison has done so by adapting familiar buildings at half the expense of new construction.

Anchor for an island

PARAMOUNT ARTS CENTRE, AURORA, ILLINOIS

When the Paramount Arts Centre opened anew in April 1978, its marquee lights broadcast the spirit of a $15-million downtown redevelopment campaign initiated by the city of Aurora, Illinois, to reverse the decline of its central business district. An industrial river town with a population of about 80,000, Aurora is located some 40 miles west of Chicago.

The Paramount itself is located on Stolp Island, a three-block parcel of land perched in the middle of the river that runs through the center of the city's downtown. Stolp and the downtown area surrounding it declined drastically in the decade between 1964 and 1974. Property values in downtown Aurora plummeted 50 percent. The dilemma was typical of that in many cities across the country during the period: merchants and their customers moved to outlying locales, and major shopping malls proved deathly competition to the deteriorating downtown buildings. The problems of Stolp Island were exacerbated by the general disrepair of the eight

bridges linking it to Aurora's other downtown areas.

In 1974 a city-funded diagnostic survey of Aurora's central and outlying areas resulted in the selection of five priority projects to stimulate downtown activity. Among the projects were the repair of Stolp's eight bridges and the purchase and renovation of the island's 1931 movie palace, the 1,900-seat Paramount Theatre designed by Rapp and Rapp.

STATE AND CITY DOLLARS FUND REDEVELOPMENT
The funding for the Paramount Arts Centre represents a fragment of a larger fiscal package in both state and city allocations. In October 1974, the Aurora city council sold $12.8 million in general obligation bonds and established a not-for-profit implementing agency, the Aurora Redevelopment Commission (ARC). The city then allocated to ARC a $4.95-million budget and assigned the agency to begin work on several projects designed to have a rapid and visible impact within the redevelopment district.

A year later, a city appeal to the Illinois State Assembly succeeded in generating legislation that created the Aurora Civic Center Authority (ACCA). The state allocated nearly $10.3 million to ACCA for development of the proposed downtown multi-use complex. Among other activities, the state monies permitted the subsequent purchase and renovation of the Paramount Theatre. The Paramount auditorium will be tied into civic center facilities as a part of the complete development package.

In spring 1976, Aurora purchased the Paramount together with the half block of adjoining storefronts for $345,000, and engaged the ELS Design Group of San Francisco as project architects. Some $2.66 million and 65,000 work hours later, the curtain opened on a reborn movie palace, replete with modern equipment successfully integrated into a polished art deco jewel.

Like many other movie palace adaptations, the renovation of the Paramount began with two primary goals: to develop a highly versatile, entirely reequipped stagehouse and stage services capable of handling the demands of diverse programming; and to upgrade authentic interior and exterior finishes, faithful expressions of the original design modified to provide the greatest possible comfort to patrons.

MAJOR CONSTRUCTION NECESSARY
Major construction was necessary to synthesize the inherited limitations of a vaudeville house and the standards of modern theater design. Backstage, a new world took shape as the shell of the stagehouse was expanded and fitted with a new stage assembly. The Paramount's location and original design facilitated improvements normally obstructed by common walls and right-of-ways. Its stagehouse was easily punctured and fortified to create 15 feet of much needed storage and crossover space. An entirely new dressing room wing was added. The stage itself was extended 12 feet and the proscenium substantially enlarged. Up-to-date sound systems and

lighting circuits were installed, as were new rigging and curtains. In addition, there was reconstruction of a facsimile marquee; hand-painted restoration of Venetian wall panels; complete refurbishing of the theater's existing seats; and salvage and repair of existing lobby fixtures, such as the art deco poster cases, panic bars, and railings.

The Paramount's facilities now rank among the most modern in the Chicago region, and a three-phase grand opening highlighted its history and future capability. The first few seasons at the Paramount have combined a range of events throughout the year, a programming strategy designed to broaden the appeal of the center. Seasonal events are scheduled back-to-back with symphony, dance, opera, children's shows, films, and touring Broadway productions.

In 1981, 80 percent of operational expenses were met by ticket sales, rentals, and other income. The facility still requires city funding support for 17 percent of its operating budget, however, and the consolidated ACCA/ARC board reports to both the Aurora city council and the state of Illinois.

Meanwhile, the Paramount Arts Centre has played a vital role in attracting new business and retail investment to Stolp Island and other areas of downtown Aurora. Improved river edge amenities, new small shops, a rejuvenated streetscape, the new North Island Civic Center Complex (of which the Paramount is a part), and other incremental projects have started to restore to the island its former preeminence.

The beautifully restored golden and red auditorium of the Paramount as it appeared on Reopening Night in 1978. The auditorium differs little from its original 1931 appearance.

City assistance makes the difference

TAMPA THEATRE, TAMPA, FLORIDA

A restored downtown movie palace is helping to revitalize Tampa's central business district by providing city and county residents with an attractive, locally programmed arts resource. In 1975 a feasibility study funded by a variety of public and private groups recommended that the city of Tampa accept title to the theater, which had been offered as a donation by its corporate owners. Although motivated primarily by the desire to save a historically significant building, the study addressed the theater's adaptive potential as a community arts facility. A year later, the city council resolved to add the 1,500-seat Tampa to its inventory of municipal properties and so undertook an ongoing restoration effort.

From a cultural facilities bond, the city allocated an initial $150,000 for the estimated $400,000 rehabilitation. The following year, the Tampa was named to the National Register of Historic Places, a designation qualifying it for a $41,000 to $51,000 service grant from the Heritage Conservation and Recreation Service of the U.S. Department of the Interior. The city in turn matched the federal grant with an additional $51,000. The Tampa Theatre Development Fund offset city expenses with a number of patron-focused promotions, including a seat endowment program. Additional restoration funds—this time in the amount of $96,000—were announced by the Tampa in 1981. (The city of Tampa matched a $48,000 grant from historic preservation funds handled by the Division of Archives, History, and Records through the U.S. Department of State.) The funds will pay for the interior restoration of the proscenium, electrical and plumbing renovations, conversion of a section of seating for the handicapped, and installation of a lift for the Mighty Wurlitzer pipe organ.

Since the Tampa's reopening, the city has carried a high percentage of the fiscal burden. Its support averages nearly $181,000 per year in operations and maintenance subsidy (1976-80 figures), approximately 55 percent of the total theater budget. (54) Still, the theater enjoys growing audiences and an ever-decreasing percentage of city funding in its operating budget.

REFLECTION OF PUBLIC ADMINISTRATION
Both the reprogramming and the restoration campaign of the Tampa Theatre, designed by John Eberson in 1926 and one of only two atmospherics in the state, reflect its public administration. The theater was reinstituted with a modest mission: "to provide space for the visual arts (primarily cinema, limited drama and exhibit/displays), enhance the image and attractiveness of downtown by generating human activity, [and] benefit the amateur artist or performer." (55) Tenacious public programming policy mandates priority (and discounted rental rates) for nonprofit arts and educational events. However, some calendar space is reserved for privately promot-

Architect's drawing of the proscenium arch and
sidewalls of the Spanish Revival Tampa Theatre
and photograph (right) showing encrusted
detailing on sidewall.

ed events, their higher rental returns designed to help lessen the dependency of the theater on city subsidies. The theater's annual programming currently features a 12- to 15-event subscription series (primarily live drama), a film society, regularly scheduled inexpensive local attractions tailored to stimulate weekday downtown business life, and special events that serve the area's various arts interests. (56)

An unusual aspect of the Tampa Theatre project is its renovation campaign and public management structure, each of which reflects both the versatility and limitations of municipally owned, small-scale arts programming. Unlike most similarly organized facilities, the Tampa has utilized the city's public works department to restore its interior, install a new mechanical plant, augment acoustical quality with modern sound equipment, fortify the electrical system, adjust lighting, and maintain service facilities. The initial eight-month restoration, accomplished with the help of innumerable volunteers (including local preservation and arts groups), witnessed the replacement of old seating and worn carpet, extensive stage repair, rehabilitation of the orchestra pit, comprehensive repainting and plasterwork, and the careful restoration of some 450 original theater artifacts. (57)

THEATER JOINTLY OPERATED
The theater is jointly operated by the City of Tampa and the Arts Council of Tampa-Hillsborough County. House staff, rental fee structure, bookings, promotion, and programming are managed and overseen by the arts council; the city provides maintenance, operating capital, and partial support from the neighboring Convention Hall staff. The full-time Tampa staff includes a director, assistant to the director, house manager, box office manager, and receptionist. Bookkeeping responsibilities have been absorbed by existing arts council and Convention Center staff.

The experience of the Tampa Theatre suggests the potential success of phased renovation, realistic programming, interagency cooperation, and a supportive public. Despite a modest if not lean budget that averaged about $330,000 between 1976 and 1980, and low renovation expenses (which reflect the limited reprogramming criteria and hidden benefits of a completely public, municipal operation), the Tampa has successfully enriched its downtown locale's architectural heritage, supplemented its contribution to the quality of life with a versatile amenity, and helped to support the Franklin Street Mall project, a local downtown revitalization effort. (58) The theater's replacement value today is nearly $2 million, and both attendance and downtown redevelopment are on the upswing.

Unparalleled in scope

PLAYHOUSE SQUARE, CLEVELAND, OHIO

Playhouse Square has no precedent in the United States,

Architect's site plan showing theater ground floor plans for Cleveland's Playhouse Square. Legend: I, Allen Theatre; 2 parking garage; 3, Ohio Theatre; 4, State Theatre; 5, Palace Theatre.

either in ambition or magnitude. As an urban redevelopment concept, it is expected to contribute more than $35 million in annual consumer spending and 500 jobs to downtown Cleveland. As an adaptive use package, it is intended to renovate and upgrade three contiguous movie palace/vaudeville theaters that can be connected to one another with existing indoor lobbies and corridors. As a performing arts center, it is planned to be the nation's single largest community of theaters, with a total seating capacity greater than either Washington's Kennedy Center or New York's Lincoln Center. As an organization, it is composed of two management arms, one profitmaking and the other nonprofit. Playhouse Square's vision for Cleveland is nothing less than the use of theaters to reinvigorate 60 acres of central city properties with a total potential reinvestment value of $118.8 million.

TRIPLE PLAY

The core of the Playhouse Square redevelopment plan is an unusual assembly of three theaters that share common walls. Each theater—the State, the Palace, and the Ohio—was constructed in 1921-22. The term Playhouse Square was coined by the press to describe Cleveland's downtown concentration of theaters. The area includes two additional theaters located outside the developmental jurisdiction of the Playhouse Square organizations, but near the theaters featured in the adaptive use proposals.

The 3,400-seat State is slated to become the flagship of the redevelopment package. Plans designate the expansion of its stagehouse to accommodate a 65-foot deep performance area with fully equipped and modern support facilities. The Cleveland Ballet and Cleveland Opera will become its chief tenants. The Palace, also with a seating capacity of 3,680, will be renovated to present concerts and other events by popular entertainers. The 1,400-seat Ohio will be refurbished as the home of the Great Lakes Shakespeare Festival and for use as a community performing arts showcase and small presentation house. Its renovation will extend the Playhouse Square facility to local arts groups and amateur or nonprofit productions. The Ohio's lobby will be redeveloped into a 350-seat dining and banquet facility, a necessary adhesive for the various entertainment areas.

Renovation work will cost $7 million at the State and $3.5 million each at the Palace and the Ohio. The Ohio's kitchen and dining rooms will add another $2.5 million to the baseline Playhouse Square investment. Plans call for the resulting entertainment center to serve as the hub of a widening revitalization effort, which will eventually encompass the entire downtown theater target renovation area. Included in the long-range plan are the renovation of office buildings, new restaurants, a hotel, and parking facilities. The tentative date for completion of the core performing arts center is early 1984, with the total estimated expenditure by completion set

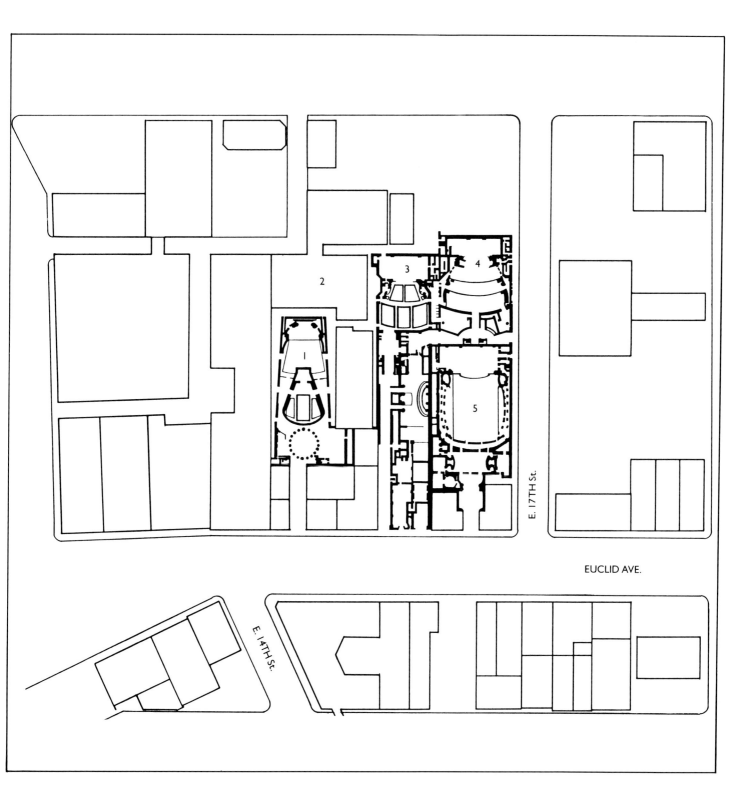

E. 17TH St.

EUCLID AVE.

E. 14TH St.

Artists' rendering of the 1929 Carolina Theatre
in Winston-Salem as it will appear in its new
life as the Roger L. Stevens Center for the Performing Arts (right), and the Carolina facade
prior to renovation (far right).

at $22.5 million. Playhouse Square programming will involve a mixed calendar of classical arts, popular entertainment, diverse touring productions, and educational and civic use.

CORE OF CITIZENS ASSEMBLES FUNDING

The Playhouse Square Foundation is a small core of Cleveland citizens organized to reverse downtown commercial decline and the resale of the theaters. Its financial structure is a complex assortment of county, city, state, federal, and private monies. Each resource has committed funds in a variety of packages to the Playhouse Square redevelopment plan. In 1977, for instance, Cuyahoga County purchased the Loew's building and its two theaters, the State and the Ohio, for $1.7 million and gave Playhouse Square responsibility for their administration. The City of Cleveland delivered nearly $3.15 million in Economic Development Administration funds to the foundation. The National Endowment for the Arts awarded a $30,000 grant to help underwrite the State Theatre reconstruction design, as well as a $500,000 challenge grant. Additional federal loans have been made and state allotments are also expected.

In addition to public money, the volunteer efforts of more than 1,000 people are valued in excess of $75,000. The private sector contributed $600,000 in operating assistance and $400,000 in absorbed expenses during the early phases of the project. Ticket sales, private restoration money and material, and individual contributions more than sustained

that phase of the project, with only one of three project theaters in operation. Corporate leadership embodied in the Greater Cleveland Growth Association has listed the Playhouse Square Foundation at the top of its priorities and big business has committed nearly $3 million to the project. Private foundations have contributed more than $2 million since the inception of the redevelopment plan. To date, Playhouse Square has raised $15 million of its $22.5-million goal.

THE FUTURE OF PLAYHOUSE SQUARE

Among the many factors that auger success for Playhouse Square is the cooperative relationship enjoyed by the Playhouse Square Foundation and the Playhouse Square Redevelopment Corporation. The not-for-profit foundation is responsible for the restoration, management, and operation of the theater cluster as a performing arts and entertainment center. The profitmaking Redevelopment Corporation is responsible for the acquisition, restoration, and operation of selected real estate properties in the Playhouse Square District. Although separate entities, the Playhouse Square Foundation is a major shareholder in the Playhouse Square Redevelopment Corporation. This relationship allows the not-for-profit organization to benefit directly from private sector development of the district to the extent that year-end profits are distributed to all shareholders.

The cycle is creatively employed to the benefit of both the

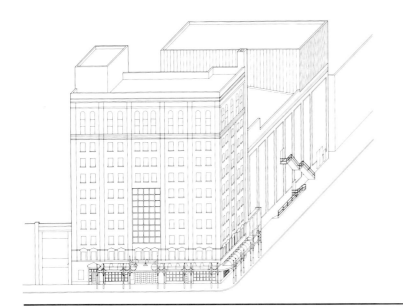

general public and local businesses: profits derived from the revitalization and economic development of the district in the end support the efforts of the nonprofit operation, which can apply any new funds to the continual upgrading and expansion of theater properties, programming, and services. In addition, the Playhouse Square Development Bank acts as a revolving fund to provide a flexible, "locally controlled development tool for property acquisition, clearance, improvements, and other forms of development guarantees and incentives." (59)

The ambitious and comprehensive vision of the Playhouse Square Foundation goes far beyond the adaptive use performing arts programming that characterizes its central activity. The foundation is an innovative force in the design of joint public/private funding strategies that can be of use to other midsized and large American cities with similarly attractive properties.

Generating regional renaissance

ROGER L. STEVENS CENTER FOR THE PERFORMING ARTS,
NORTH CAROLINA SCHOOL OF THE ARTS,
WINSTON-SALEM, NORTH CAROLINA

The best place to feel the pulse of $100 million in new development now taking place in downtown Winston-Salem is at its heart: a 1920s movie palace called the Carolina

Theatre. The theater first encountered the vision and imagination of the North Carolina School of the Arts (NCSA) in 1971, and in 1982—a decade later—after a $9.5-million transformation, the Carolina will unloose its wings as the Roger L. Stevens Center for the Performing Arts. (The center is named in honor of the Board Chairman of Washington's Kennedy Center. Mr. Stevens also served as the first Chairman of the National Endowment for the Arts and is a former NCSA Board member.)

To say the least, NCSA's program for the Roger L. Stevens Center is ambitious. First and foremost, the facility has been redesigned to function as the school's primary professional training ground for all facets of theatrical production—a multiple-purpose performing arts laboratory fully equipped with mainstream, state-of-the-art technology. Second, it will serve as a showcase roadhouse for the southeastern United States, capable of satisfying the requirements for full-scale Broadway presentations. Third, the theater will be the permanent home of the Winston-Salem Symphony Orchestra, the Piedmont Chamber Orchestra, and the North Carolina Dance Theatre.

CAMPUS BUILT AROUND FOUND SPACE
The NCSA, chartered by an act of the state legislature in 1963 and added to North Carolina's sixteen-school University System in 1971, has built an entire campus for its 600 students around found space. (Among the half dozen aban-

Architect's drawing of street level plan, Roger L. Stevens Center. Legend: 1, marquee; 2, greenhouse; 3, entrance lobby; 4, restaurant; 5, kitchen; 6, artist warm-up.

Architect's drawing of orchestra level plan, Roger L. Stevens Center. Legend: 7, exterior porch; 8, orchestra lobby; 9, orchestra; 10, stage. (Facing page.)

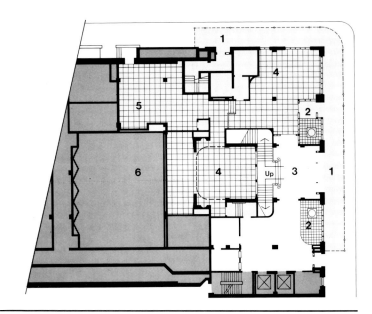

doned buildings it has converted into classroom space are a 1929 high school and its 1943 gymnasium addition, a diaper laundry, a World War II spring factory, a brake shop, and a five-acre, 63,000 square foot truck sales and service complex.) In 1972, when NCSA's quantum growth led the institution to cast its net for new performance space, found space again seemed a likely candidate.

NCSA development director Samuel M. Stone explained to the school's Board of Trustees that the Carolina, its structural integrity verified by state engineers, could be renovated to meet NCSA needs at a cost far lower than that of new construction. The Trustees' primary concern, however, focused on the Carolina's location: a mile from NCSA's campus and in the center of an economically beleaguered downtown business district known for its crime and parking problems. After months of debate, the Board agreed to commission a study on the feasibility of transforming the Carolina into a major performing arts center.

The first structural evaluations corroborated early intuitions about the potential of the theater. Acquisition of the property, however, was another issue. Initially, the school had hoped to persuade the city of Winston-Salem to purchase the Carolina and then lease it back to NCSA for reconstruction and reprogramming. At the time, the theater was owned by Piedmont Publishing Company, producers of Winston-Salem's daily morning and evening newspapers. Piedmont,

like NCSA, anticipated expansion and was holding the theater property as contingency real estate. In an unanticipated turn of events, the city council agreed to sell Piedmont municipal land adjacent to its current offices. Piedmont, in turn, donated the theater to the school at an assessed value of $345,000.

CONVERSION OF THE CAROLINA THEATRE

The Carolina Theatre was designed in 1929 by architects Stanhope Johnson and R.O. Bannan of Lynchburg, Virginia. The theater is the core of an 11-story apartment-turned-hotel development, which features an understated renaissance revival motif. In converting the Carolina to a performing arts center, project architects faced more obstacles than opportunities. Nananne Porcher, principal in the New Jersey theater consulting firm of Jean Rosenthal Associates, a NCSA faculty member and consultant for the renovation project, explains:

Although it had a decent commercial auditorium for showing movies, the theater's mezzanine and balcony were gigantic, far too large for the school's needs. Acoustics were a disaster. The lobby was nearly nonexistent, basically a pass-through. To make matters worse, the stage was built eight feet below street level, a treacherous loading problem.

The architects, Newman Calloway Johnson Winfree, of Winston-Salem, were unwilling to succumb to the building's

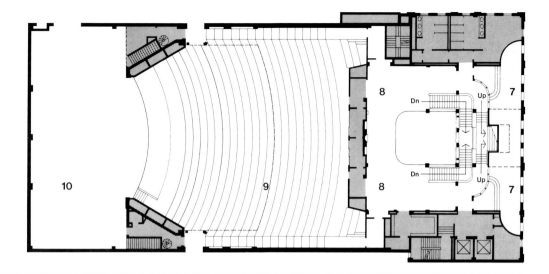

limitations, and initiated one innovative solution after another. First, they addressed the problem of stage service. By completely removing the mezzanine and lower balcony, raising the stage to street level, and then raising the orchestra level to suit the new stage height, space was created under the orchestra and stage floor to accommodate 22 artist dressing rooms, two chorus dressing rooms, pit storage, wardrobe, scene shops, a large rehearsal area, and other critical services. This reconstruction allowed the installation of a 95-seat orchestra pit, and significantly improved the acoustical quality of the house. In addition, the stage was extended six feet beyond the outer edge of the proscenium opening to accommodate greater production capacity and create cross-over space in the rear-stage area. The stagehouse was raised 10 feet and reroofed in conjunction with new rigging and gridiron requirements.

Acoustical panels at the rear and sides of the stage will enrich stage-mounted symphony concerts and opera productions. A scallop-shell forestage sound reflector installed overhead will also support a variety of special lighting assemblies. In addition, the theater will employ a sound system to assist patrons with impaired hearing. (Sound waves will be translated into infrared frequencies and transmitted to wireless headsets that allow patrons in need of the service to sit anywhere in the house.)

The removal of the second floor over the old lobby and the installation of a grand staircase has synchronized circulation with the design of the new auditorium. A spacious orchestra lobby, located on the second level, will connect to a third-level, four-story smoking porch. Two elevators will service all upper floors and a restaurant is planned for the residual space left at ground level just beyond the remodeled entranced lobby. Offices for NCSA department heads will be located on the theater's fourth floor and linked to stage and theater activity by intercom and closed-circuit television hookups. Additional floors will be utilized to house the adult music education program, which requires separate recital halls and music rooms. An apartment/office combination seems the most likely of several alternative plans under consideration for developing the remaining five stories of the complex.

IMPRESSIVE FUNDING ASSORTMENT

Funding for the Roger L. Stevens Center is no less impressive than projected plans for the theater's metamorphosis. It represents the involvement of a host of multinational corporations, private developers, city officials, internationally acclaimed performing artists, and three separate federal agencies. In 1978, the Economic Development Administration (EDA) awarded NCSA $100,000 to conduct the initial feasibility study. NCSA then received $293,000 as part of a $700,000 National Endowment for the Arts challenge grant awarded to a consortium of local arts organizations. In 1979, NCSA

On the stage of the Carolina, designers confer with representatives from the North Carolina School of the Arts about new use for the old theater.

received a second EDA allocation of $3.14 million, which will help to pay restoration expenses. The same year, the school received a $275,000 grant from the U.S. Department of the Interior Appalachian Regional Commission.

R.J. Reynolds Industries, a Winston-Salem-based corporation, heads an impressive roster of private contributors with a $1.2 million gift. Exxon, Celanese/Fiber Industries, Hanes Corporation, Hanes Dye and Finishing Company, Union Carbide, the Bell System, IBM, Alcoa, Mobil, Phillip Morris, Koppers, and Wachovia Bank and Trust have each helped to fuel the center's future. Not one cent of the North Carolina University System's educational funds have been spent, although the University will contribute to the operating expenses of the facility.

NCSA's move into downtown Winston-Salem has had an astonishing impact on the city's central business district. In response to the school's activity, a local developer purchased an old J.C. Penny building across the street from the Carolina. After $1.9 million of renovation and upgrading, the building —now used for office space—is doing strong business. Around the corner, an $18-million, 18-story office complex was recently completed.

ARTS COUNCIL DEVELOPS MAJOR URBAN PARK NEARBY
On an adjoining block, the Arts Council of Winston-Salem has developed "Winston Square," a $4-million arts-related redevelopment project. In addition to the renovation and reuse of

a historic textile mill, Winston Square will feature the city's first major urban park, designed to mix an open amphitheater with many other outdoor amenities. Altogether, $34 million —$13 million of which is arts-related—has been invested in the three-square-block area that surrounds the theater. Citywide, the total reinvestment resulting in large part from the vision and daring of the NCSA/Carolina Theatre venture is staggering—$100 million in private development completed, committed, or underway.

The new 1,385-seat Roger L. Stevens Center for the Performing Arts will officially open on April 22, 1983, followed by a week-long gala featuring actors Gregory Peck and Charlton Heston, actress and Winston-Salem native Rosemary Harris, conductor Leonard Bernstein, and violinist Isaac Stern. Roger L. Stevens, of course, also will be in attendance. Distinguished alumni of NCSA, representing many of the nation's eminent performing arts organizations, will return to help celebrate the latest achievement of their alma mater. Among the other stars of the event: the artists whose names have not yet appeared in lights—NCSA's current and future students.

THE OTHER TWO-THIRDS

Ernest Hemingway suggested that the dignity of an iceberg

derives from the fact that seven-eighths of its mass is hidden under water. The preceding case studies represent only a fraction—about one-third—of the total number of movie palaces across the United States restored or adapted for new use.

From other notable projects, the following 30 have been selected to demonstrate the magnitude of this national trend. The list includes movie palaces as well as vaudeville and legitimate theaters, and represents projects in various stages of work—some completed, others ongoing, and still others on the drawing boards. Although the locales, styles, and costs of the projects differ, one consideration remains constant: older theaters are a widely recognized cultural, social, and economic asset with deeply rooted meaning for those communities fortunate enough to benefit from their survival. While some of the movie palace renaissance themes already have been discussed, we also introduce new themes in this section, particularly the reuse of theaters for purposes other than the performing arts.

Akron, Ohio: The Akron Civic Theater (formerly Loew's, John Eberson, 1929) has been owned and operated by the Community Hall Foundation since 1965. One of the first theaters built with sound equipment for "talkies," the multiple-purpose performing arts facility is considered a vital component of downtown Akron redevelopment. Public financing and private contributions continue to finance ongoing technical improvements and restoration.

Boston, Massachusetts: Originally a flagship vaudeville theater, later a movie palace, the Savoy (formerly B.F. Keith, Thomas Lamb, 1928) now is home for Sarah Caldwell's Opera Company of Boston. Purchased by the organization in 1978, the Savoy has undergone extensive cosmetic restoration: cleansing and rewiring; enlarging the orchestra pit; removing a concrete wall that blocked the proscenium; and installing the company's administrative offices, costume department, and scene shop. Projects still on the company's drawing boards: extending the stage depth from 33 feet to 75 feet; restoring the auditorium to its original splendor; installing up-to-date stage rigging (none of the original remains); refurbishing dressing rooms; and eventually enlarging backstage areas to accommodate rehearsal rooms and a projected full-scale school for training young opera performers, directors, and technicians.

Bridgeport, Connecticut: The not-for-profit P.T. Barnum Center was established in late 1980 for the purpose of acquiring and renovating two older theaters, the Majestic and the Palace, as a performing arts complex. The project profits from the active support of the Connecticut Grand Opera Association and the Shakespeare Theatre of Stratford, as well as local architects, attorneys, and other public-spirited citizens.

Buffalo, New York: The municipally funded $770,000 restoration of the Shea's Buffalo (Rapp and Rapp, 1926) is part of an ambitious development concept designed to reinvigorate the city's theater district, an area covering 106 acres

A drawing of the magnificent white terra-cotta facade of the 1927 Indiana Theatre in Indianapolis. The ornamentation features portrait medallions of King Ferdinand and Queen Isabella of Spain and a sundial (top right).

adjacent to Buffalo's central business district. Long-range plans call for mixing a variety of cultural and entertainment activities with related private investment, new light-rail public transportation, major urban improvements, and related adaptive use/restoration projects.

Canton, Ohio: The 1,875-seat Palace Theatre (John Eberson, 1926) was reopened in 1980 for movies, stage productions, concerts, lectures, and meetings. The project's success is due largely to the efforts of the Canton Palace Theatre Association, a not-for-profit organization chartered to preserve the local landmark and provide it with a second life. Volunteers and a modest paid staff manage and operate the theater.

Cedar Rapids, Iowa: The renaissance of the Paramount Theatre for the Performing Arts is due in part to the generosity of two local residents who provided funds for the city to purchase the 1,900-seat movie palace (formerly the Capital, Peacock and Frank, 1928). Private donations have supported restoration work and technical improvements for the theater, which reopened in 1976 with a diverse performing arts calendar.

Chicago, Illinois: Once the entertainment and movie mecca of its Southside neighborhood, the Avalon (John Eberson, 1927) was adapted by a local religious organization for use as a church. Since 1970, the giant Middle Eastern atmospheric theater has served its congregation as the Miracle Temple.

Dayton, Ohio: The Victory Theatre, a legitimate house built in 1919, has been operated by the Victory Theatre Association as a performing arts center since 1975. A recent $350,000 donation will help the organization complete its purchase of the landmark and launch a $375,000 fundraising campaign for continued restoration.

Fort Wayne, Indiana: Under the management of the Embassy Theatre Foundation (assisted by public support, private donations, active programming, and the Fort Wayne Redevelopment Commission), the Embassy Theatre enjoyed a healthy 1980-81 season of diverse performing arts events. Fundraising helped to reduce the principal debt of the restored movie palace, which now serves as home for the Fort Wayne Philharmonic, by $25,000.

Indianapolis, Indiana: Over $5 million has been invested in reconstruction of the Indiana Repertory Theatre (formerly the Indiana, Rubush & Hunter, 1927), which reopened in 1980. The old movie palace was transformed into a state-of-the-art cultural complex which includes three separate performance areas, rehearsal space, storage and service area, and Rep offices. Local trusts, municipal support, and grants from the National Endowment for the Arts contributed to the successful project, which represents the heart of downtown redevelopment plans.

Ithaca, New York: The Strand, an 1,100-seat 1917 vaudeville house, was saved from demolition in 1977 by the Tompkins County Center for Culture and the Performing

Rear view of Reverend Ike's United Church in New York, clad in terra-cotta and brick. The front of the 1928 cathedral-like structure, originally the Loew's 175th Street Theatre, includes space for commercial tenants.

Arts. The center received invaluable assistance and support from U.S. Army Reserve volunteers, Cornell University fraternities, and Ithaca's mayor. The theater was reopened in 1977, and restoration plans have proceeded hand-in-hand with active arts programming and special events, including dance, jazz, theatre, and performances by local opera, chamber music, and ballet groups.

Kansas City, Missouri: Restoration of the Folly Theatre, a 1900 vaudeville playhouse, is approaching completion. Saved from destruction for a parking lot by enthusiastic public support, the local landmark will reopen as a performing arts facility, the most recent of many transformations in its 80-year history.

Los Angeles, California: Patterned after the colorful atmosphere of an Eastern bazaar, the transformation of the downtown Pantages (B. Marcus Priteca, 1921) remains among the most successful retail conversions of old movie palaces. After securing a lease on the property in 1977 with an option to buy, a local entrepreneur generated advance funds from 75 local merchants and began converting the theater into what is now the Theater Jewelry Centre. The eventual $2.1-million purchase of the theater included the nine-story building in which it is housed. An additional $1.7 million was spent reconditioning the space, flattening the orchestra floor, and replacing and repairing mechanical systems. Today, 135 booths occupy three levels in one of the city's most active jewelry marts.

Marion, Ohio: Yet another Ohio atmospheric (formerly the Palace, John Eberson, 1928) was reborn in 1978 after the not-for-profit Palace Cultural Arts Association led a restoration rally that brought together private and public supporters. Today, the Palace Theatre offers a community-based performing arts program.

New York, New York: When it reopens in 1982, the intimate 450-seat Elgin Theater, a small Art Deco movie house, will be the country's first arts facility devoted to the exclusive year-round performance of dance. A private contribution by one of its board members enabled the Eliot Feld Ballet to purchase the theater in 1979. Since then, a combination of private financing and state and federal grants—a total package of $3.5 million—will support capital and operating costs.

Another New York movie palace, the Loew's Valencia (John Eberson, 1929), was donated by its owners to the Pentecostal Church in 1977. Since then, Eberson's fanciful neoclassical statues have been clothed and winged and the lobby walls now display the crutches of the healed.

Also in New York, the United Church purchased and converted the Loew's 175th Street Theatre (Thomas Lamb, 1930) into a 3,500-seat cathedral for the ministry of Frederick Eikerenkoetter (Reverend Ike). Restoration and capital development funds were raised by the church congregation.

Omaha, Nebraska: A feasibility study was commissioned in 1980 to explore reuse scenarios for the Astro (formerly the Riviera, John Eberson, 1927), a 2,800-seat movie palace

Pittsburgh's Penn Theatre, a 1927 movie palace
(right) transformed in 1971 into Heinz Hall,
a French Renaissance showcase (far right). The
marquee was removed in restoration, revealing
the classical elegance of the Beaux Arts facade.

which local preservationists hope to link to nearby down-town redevelopment activity. The study calls for a mixed-use, multiple-purpose programming concept that will complement the city's investment in a refreshed central business district.

Pittsburgh, Pennsylvania: After a $10-million reconstruction program, the Pittsburgh Loew's Penn reopened in 1971 as Heinz Hall, a gem in the nationally recognized renaissance of the city's Golden Triangle. The 1927 Rapp and Rapp French Renaissance showcase had been transformed into a 19th-century music hall to meet the acoustical requirements of the Pittsburgh Symphony Society, its new owner, and its 3,486-seat capacity reduced to seat 2,847 patrons more comfortably. In addition to the Pittsburgh Symphony, Heinz Hall resident companies include the Pittsburgh Ballet, Pittsburgh Opera, Pittsburgh Civic Light Opera, Pittsburgh Youth Symphony, and Pittsburgh Dance Council. Over 275 events are booked annually in the hall, including performances by its resident companies as well as Broadway touring productions and entertainers such as Lena Horne.

During the past three years, the success of Heinz Hall has prompted extensive additional capital improvements, notably the construction of new lobby space, kitchen facilities, an expanded box office, and a private dining club. Outside, a new public park with fountain and water sculpture is enjoyed by Heinz Hall patrons and the general public.

Portland, Oregon: Voters recently approved a local bond issue that will add a restored Paramount Theatre (Rapp and Rapp, 1928) to the Portland Performing Arts Complex. The restoration of the extravagant 3,000-seat movie palace will provide a home base for the Portland Symphony Orchestra and other performing arts activities.

Poughkeepsie, New York: In 1976, the oldest opera house in New York State and the seventh oldest in the country was facing replacement by a parking lot. Today, the historic Bardavon 1869 Opera House is a flourishing multiple-purpose performing arts facility. Ongoing restoration work is funded by donations and subscription memberships, and the restoration and reprogramming of the theater is now considered a major force in the reanimation of downtown Poughkeepsie.

Providence, Rhode Island: The Ocean State Performing Arts Center (formerly the Loew's State, Rapp and Rapp, 1928) was privately restored in 1976, two years before a locally initiated feasibility study resulted in the purchase of the theater by its current not-for-profit management. The Rhode Island Historical Preservation Commission, the Mayor's Office of Community Development, and seven local businesses contributed nearly $800,000 for facility improvements, enabling the OSPAC project to go forward in 1978.

Richmond, Virginia: The Virginia Center for the Performing Arts is gearing up for a $6-million fundraising drive to transform the 2,100-seat Loew's Richmond (John Eberson,

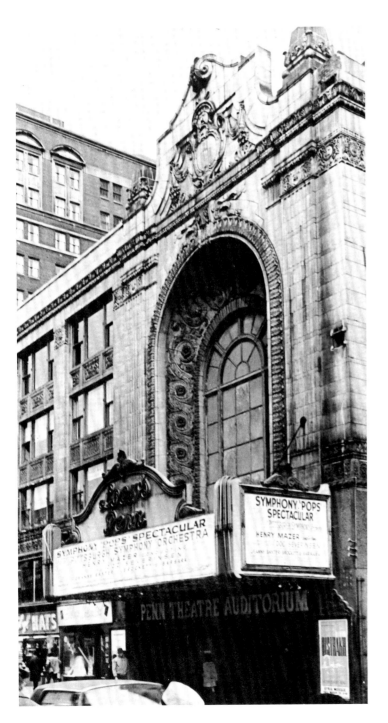

Architect's conceptual rendering of a performing arts event at one of several theaters in the proposed San Antonio Performing Arts District.

1928) into a new cultural facility for the area. The handsome Moorish/Spanish Colonial Revival theater also will serve as the new home of the Richmond Symphony, which will add its name to a growing list of orchestra associations that have found new homes in old movie palaces.

Salt Lake City, Utah: Since 1978, Utah's Ballet West, the Repertory Dance Theatre, the Ririe-Woodbury Dance Company, and the Utah Opera Company have shared facilities in the Capital Theater (formerly the Orpheum, G. Albert Landsburgh, 1913). Restored and expanded at a cost of $4.5 million, the 1,942-seat vaudeville house constitutes a third component of the city's new downtown cultural facilities, which include the Utah Symphony Hall and Salt Lake City Art Center.

San Antonio, Texas: After a promising feasibility study completed in 1979, work continues on the organization of the San Antonio Performing Arts District, an urban redevelopment concept that revolves around the restoration and reprogramming of three neighboring theaters, two of which were designed as movie palaces. Similar in concept to Cleveland's Playhouse Square, the San Antonio Arts plan calls for the consolidation of management and facilities for the city's many performing arts organizations.

St. Joseph, Missouri: In 1977, city residents approved a $750,000 bond issue which enabled St. Joseph to purchase and renovate the Missouri Theater (Boller Brothers, 1927) as a performing arts center. Over $400,000 in preliminary im-

provements have been supported by an ongoing campaign to raise funds for upgraded services, new stage equipment, and phased building restoration.

St. Louis, Missouri: A diverse coalition of midtown St. Louis arts, education, civic, religious, and financial institutions joined forces in 1980 to serve as stockholders of City Center Redevelopment Corp. Their goal: to bring the midtown district back to life.

At the heart of City Center's long-range planning scenario is a flourishing midtown economy supported by four performing arts facilities, including Powell Symphony Hall, the giant 5,000-seat Fox Theater (C. Howard Crane, 1929), the 1,200-seat Lyn (originally a vaudeville and burlesque house), and the 1912 Sheldon Memorial, a neoclassical music hall.

The Fox, recently purchased by the city's largest private redevelopment company, will be restored to accommodate events ranging from popular entertainment and Broadway shows to grand opera. The Lyn is well-suited for ballet and repertory film. The Sheldon Memorial, yet a smaller auditorium, will augment the other facilities with programs of chamber music, recitals, and special events.

Financing of City Center calls for $3 million in capital improvements publicly financed, $6 million in philanthropic funds, and $30 million in privately financed commercial and residential investment.

Syracuse, New York: In 1977, the Loew's State (Thomas Lamb, 1928) was about to fall victim to a shopping center/

The magnificent cast iron facade of Wilmington's restored Grand Opera House.

parking lot complex when public interest and historic designation saved it from demolition. Today, the Syracuse Area Landmark Theatre is home to special events and diverse performing arts programming while restoration continues.

Tacoma, Washington: The 1918 Roxy (formerly the Pantages, B. Marcus Priteca), a vaudeville/movie palace, was purchased by the City of Tacoma and will be transformed as the Pantages Center for the Performing Arts Fundraising efforts continue in support of the theater's full restoration, the completion of which will provide the southern Puget Sound area with a new showcase for cultural events.

Tarrytown, New York: The 1885 Music Hall was rescued from an uncertain future by the Friends of the Mozartina Musical Arts Conservatory, a local music school. Fundraising campaigns in 1980 generated $40,000 to secure a mortgage on the historic structure, which will be programmed to house concerts, plays, dance recitals, special interest events, and classic film repertory.

Youngstown, Ohio: The generosity of several local citizens predicated a community-wide effort to save the lavish rococo Warner Theater (Rapp and Rapp, 1931) from demolition and provide the Youngstown Symphony with a permanent, 2,360-seat home. Since its restoration in 1969, Powers Auditorium has not only provided the community with an important cultural asset, but preserved a significant footnote in the city's history. The Warner brothers, born and raised in Youngstown, originally built the sound-equipped movie palace in memory of their brother, Sam, and their parents.

The list of restored, reprogrammed, and relit theaters goes on. The Saenger Theater in New Orleans, the Grand Opera House in Wilmington, Delaware, and the Pabst Theater in Milwaukee lead the list in terms of size and grandeur. Smaller—but equally important—houses have been reanimated in South Bend, Indiana; Manchester, New Hampshire; Miami, Florida; Dubuque, Iowa; Denver, Colorado; and other locales nationwide. In some cities, such as Columbus, Ohio, and Richmond, Virginia, the success of pathfinding movie palace projects has stimulated coattail restorations in other areas of the city or region.

Tomorrow promises to witness the rise of a hundred movie palace curtains—testaments to the demonstrated success of projects already completed, as well as the excitement promoted by others on the drawing boards today.

RELIGHTING
THE MARQUEE

From the first exchange of ideas to the lighting of the marquee on opening night, every adapted movie palace embodies the implementation of a plan. Planning is a means of establishing goals, using resources well, and rallying support. It will help implement programs that can transform an old and perhaps abandoned movie palace into a vital element of community life. It is important that planning for the reuse of a movie palace be consciously and logically undertaken. Because the vast majority of movie palace reuse projects involve reuse as performing arts centers, we concentrate here on suggestions to help you meet the ultimate challenge: lighting a marquee not only on opening night, but also on nights for years to come.

GOING PUBLIC, AND OTHER ORGANIZATIONAL OPTIONS

With movie palaces, as with most other adaptive use efforts, (71) the organization of money and management is centralized within a single decision-making entity whose size and structure are defined by the project's specific goals. A theater reuse effort may begin as a not-for-profit venture, a private profitmaking enterprise, or a governmental undertaking. Each economic formula calls for different operational strategies, based on the circumstances surrounding property acquisition, improvement, and reprogramming. In any case, the organization charged with managing all phases of a reprogrammed theater's operations—from purchase to payroll—must be tailored to fulfill its original and ongoing objectives.

Not-for-profit corporations represent the most typical management structure of adapted movie palaces. Because most theaters continue to be reprogrammed for use as performing arts facilities, the not-for-profit format is particularly beneficial to funding. The organization of a nonprofit corporation generally begins with the covenant of its board of directors. As the 1965 Rockefeller Panel Report on the Performing Arts emphasized, a board of directors is

. . . . vested with the responsibility of maintaining and expanding the organization and has certain obvious functions: to determine the larger objectives of the organization, to retain the best available artistic direction and business management and, having done this, to back their judgment. In fulfilling these responsibilities the board has a pressing obligation to make certain the institution has financial stability. (60)

To this end, the selection and subsequent appointment of a board should represent the best available assembly of influence, expertise, and resources in each area of the undertaking.

(*Preceding page*) Powell Symphony Hall—
formerly the St. Louis Theatre—on Opening
Night, 1968.

Patrons arrive for an evening of music at
Pittsburgh's Heinz Hall following its conversion from the Penn Theatre. The
Penn was purchased by the nonprofit
Pittsburgh Symphony Society for use by
the Symphony and other Pittsburgh
arts groups.

The board often establishes a committee system to pursue each phase of project development—financing, construction, programming, facility management, and general operations, for example. It also selects a paid executive director or manager who executes its policies and manages the day-to-day theater operations. Additional staff, paid or volunteer, full- or part-time, may include an assistant director, stage manager, development and public relations director, and clerical and custodial personnel.

The majority of nonprofit theater reuse projects qualify for tax-exempt status under Section 50l(c)(3) of the Internal Revenue Code (as specified in the 1976 Tax Reform Act). The most important aspect of this classification is its inherent fundraising advantage. With tax-exempt status, an organization is allowed to solicit private tax-deductible contributions from the entire spectrum of citizens, businesses, and corporations, both locally and nationwide. Such fundraising leverage allows the immediate implementation of campaign strategies to support project start-up costs. For instance, tickets for events, as well as in-kind services, can qualify as partially tax-deductible.

Profitmaking corporations will no doubt be an increasingly attractive organizational option for theater renaissance in the 1980s. The Economic Recovery Tax Act of 1981 created major new incentives to encourage the preservation and reuse of historic buildings, including a 25 percent investment tax credit. The legal structure of the private corporation can take many forms. However, in most cases (such as the Arlington Center for the Performing Arts in Santa Barbara), the acquisition and reuse of a movie palace will be absorbed in a larger corporate enterprise and thereby inherit that corporation's existing decision-making apparatus. In other cases (Playhouse Square in Cleveland and the 5th Avenue in Seattle), private and not-for-profit enterprise can form invaluable partnerships, dividing ownership and operation with separate incorporated branches of a single theater project.

*Governments—municipal and regional—*can also purchase, restore, adapt, and operate movie palaces. In Madison, Yakima, and Tampa, for instance, adapted movie palaces are managed as a part of the municipal building inventory. The "by-the-people, for-the-people" theater reuse format can either create its own organization through local or state legislation, or become part of government structure. In either option, existing governmental resources can be used in project implementation and management.

Public agencies can often prove especially useful partners in movie palace reuse ventures because they exist in part to oversee the interests of the community in general. Building codes, zoning restrictions, ancillary services, and tax programs all fall under the aegis of such civic authority, and successful completion of a project requires cooperation in these areas.

The Avalon Theatre in New York City, now a church.

Educational and religious institutions have purchased old movie palaces for a variety of new uses. In Milwaukee, for instance, a vocational school operates from a movie palace/retail complex, and New York's Long Island University purchased an old theater for conversion to a gymnasium. As in private and municipal development, operation of such adapted theaters, regardless of use, relies on existing organizational hierarchies.

In Chicago, New York City, and other cities, large theaters have been purchased by a variety of religious congregations to serve as churches and temples, a far less expensive alternative than new construction. In these cases, organizational structure already was in place and fundraising was engineered by church members.

STARTING PLAYERS: ASSEMBLING THE DEVELOPMENT TEAM

Once sponsor and facility are established, the renaissance of a movie palace can flourish as an organized effort. *Organization* will influence the success of the project, and a strong development team can function as its nucleus.

The team should include individuals who can synchronize the variety of skills and activities requisite to attract wide-spread community support—both moral and financial—for the project. Professional team members might include:

☐ an architect to plan and direct adaptive reuse of the theater

☐ an architectural historian to research the theater's building history (including information on its original architect and architectural significance) and recommend specific areas for preservation and restoration

☐ an attorney to expedite theater acquisition and advise on insurance and other legal issues

☐ an economic analyst to conduct financial feasibility studies and prepare reports on target markets

☐ electrical, mechanical, and structural engineers to assess the theater's physical condition

☐ a fundraiser to research and solicit funding sources

☐ a general director of personnel, planning services, and other broad areas of adaptive reuse and, later, programming

☐ a public relations specialist to publicize the project by means of special events and media coverage.

Undoubtedly, the team will turn to other specialists (such as acousticians, contractors, graphic artists, interior designers, and stage technicians) as the project unfolds. The number of individuals consulted—for some areas of responsibility overlap one another—will likely be determined by the project's complexity and financial reserves.

Architect's elevation and section drawings for Wilmington's Grand Opera House showed clearly how the facade (top) would appear and space would be used (bottom) following the facility's 1975 restoration.

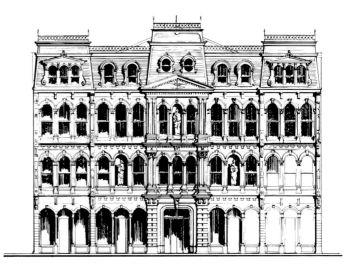

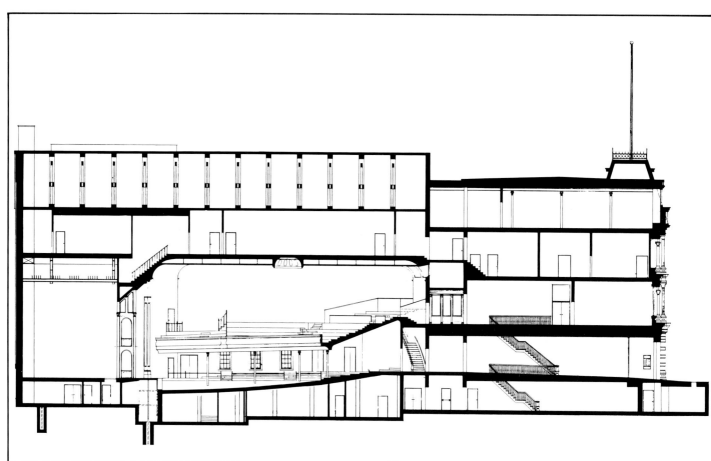

Restored lobby of the United Artists Theatre in Chicago, illustrating common components of movie palace auditoriums: balconies, ornamental side walls, organ grilles flanking the proscenium, orchestra pit, stage, and curtain assemblies.

LOOKING UNDER THE DUST

The early evaluation of a theater's condition and capacity for adaptation is the most critical step in the process that leads toward the relighted marquee. Measured against development objectives, a realistic property assessment will affect cost estimates, market analysis, feasibility studies, planning, improvements, and operation. Because adaptive reuse alternatives rely on the synthesis of these issues, the initial diagnosis of the theater and its potential involves close scrutiny—literally, looking under the dust.

A movie palace is a special breed of building originally designed to satisfy a fairly rigid theatrical program. Variations in size and architectural motif notwithstanding, seating, sight lines, and stage organization developed to support a hybrid format of live entertainment were constructed with common components. These include:

- a self-advertising, high-profile facade
- an electric marquee and vertical sign
- an enclosed or protected outer lobby with ticket booth
- a grand inner lobby
- an embellished stair serving balcony seating areas
- a projection booth
- an auditorium
- ornamented sidewalls
- organ grilles, flanking a proscenium arch
- an orchestra pit
- a stage
- curtain assemblies
- a stagehouse containing gridiron, bridges, and rigging
- dressing rooms
- heating, ventilating, and air-conditioning systems.

First, the basic structural integrity of the building must be examined closely. Past experience indicates that movie palaces are unusually strong, durable, and well-constructed buildings. Nonetheless, every detail of their inner workings —material condition, electrical network and wiring (including stage-related lighting), plumbing layout, heating, ventilating, and air-conditioning systems, roof, windows and window frames, fixtures and hardware, decorative elements, flooring, rigging systems, stagehouse construction, and all doors—should be carefully and systematically inspected in the fashion of a complete inventory of existing parts. This inventory will prove useful in the structure's authentic restoration, purchasing of insurance, value assessment, and cost estimates. On the basis of this initial inventory, all other work related to the theater restoration and renovation project will proceed.

Seating for the Brown Grand Theatre auditorium was donated by a nearby college at which the older seats were being replaced by newer furnishings.

The grand lobby of the 1927 Uptown Theatre in Chicago (shown here in an early photograph) would provide commodious space for a small cafe, champagne reception, elegant pre-theater dinner, or other performance-related activities.

AREAS OF FUNCTION

A theater can be divided into four areas of function involving various categories of occupancy and use: audience, performance, technology, and management. Each area works in concert with the others. The preliminary analysis of a property should carefully explore each of these functions: the needs of those they support, their space and technical requirements, and the manner in which they can be integrated, as well as all needed repairs, improvements, and alterations.

Audience

Spacially, functionally, programmatically, and economically, the patron is the most important occupant of the theater. Audience needs and comfort involve any part of the theater patrons use or can see. Key audience-related issues include:

Outer lobby, ticket sales, and entry. What is the size of the outer lobby and will it accommodate crowds waiting for admission to the auditorium? Is the area indoors or otherwise protected from inclement weather? Is it visible and easy to identify from the street? Where is the location of the ticket booth in relationship to the theater entrance and outer lobby?

Grand inner lobby. Will the lobby comfortably accommodate intermission activity? Is there adequate space for a small cafe area, displays, or special events? Where are restrooms, telephone, and refreshment areas located?

Circulation. Are doors and exit signs easy to locate? Will aisles satisfy emergency exit code requirements? Are stairs and railings intact? Are there provisions for handicapped patrons?

Seating arrangement and sight lines. What is the style and condition of the theater seating arrangement? What are the back-to-back dimensions between rows of seats? What percentage of seating is located in balcony areas? Would continental (side aisles only) or conventional seating be preferable? Are sight lines adequate for the proposed programmed use of the facility?

Life safety systems. In the event of an emergency, will the theater provide adequate protection for the audience? Is the sprinkler system operable and up to code? Is standing room safe and authorized by local fire codes?

Auditorium lighting. Is lighting adequate to provide for the safe movement of the patrons before, during, and after a performance?

Performance

An audience comes to the theater for entertainment, educa-

Chandelier in the Riverside Theatre, Milwaukee. Such lighting fixtures throughout movie palaces require the regular replacement of thousands of bulbs.

tion, and cultural experience. Production requirements stageside of the proscenium arch will depend largely on the specific use, type of event, and general programming philosophy of the theater's sponsor. The following stage-related areas will require close attention if the theater is intended to support live performance of any kind.

Proscenium opening and curtain assemblies. Is it the original opening? Is there an opportunity to expand the size of the opening without interfering with existing ornament, decor, or structure?

Stage. Is its size adequate? (The average movie palace stage measures 30 by 60 feet.) What is the type and condition of stage flooring? Is there adequate crossover space at the rear of the stage? How deep are the wings? Do right-of-ways or property lines prohibit stage expansion? Where are the stage doors? Are there loading facilities? What is the quality of space located underneath the stage?

Dressing rooms. How many are there? Where are they located? Will security be a problem? Is there a star dressing room and chorus dressing room? Do dressing rooms have plumbing? How many restrooms and showers serve the performers' preparation area? Does an opportunity exist to augment or expand dressing room areas?

Rehearsal space, set and costume design shops, storage, and auxiliary stage service. How much auxiliary space is available for the integration of a green room, set prepara-

tion, support for the activities of performers and backstage crew, and other production activities?

Technology

Every aspect of theater design and operation is supported by an elaborate technological system. In older theaters, technology is particularly vulnerable to age. Heating, ventilating, and air-conditioning systems are usually antiquated. Behind every light bulb in the theater (expect to encounter thousands, if not tens of thousands), a 50-year-old wire may be hiding. Stage lighting is often inadequate, if usable. The stage is a veritable science of rigging with its pinrails, ropes, lines, and catwalks. The rigging, vulnerable to age, is usually inadequate for modern productions. Most theaters adapted for multiple-purpose performing arts activities will also require acoustical amplification and sound systems.

The restoration or replacement of technology—the heart of the secrets of theater—is a high-cost category with a long list of line items on any restoration budget. Technical diagnosis, therefore, must be particularly attentive to detail. In assessing a theater's mechanical systems, for instance, determine the condition of ductwork, intake and supply vents, and the boiler. In reviewing auditorium and circulation electrical systems, determine the number and type of fixtures, and location of controls, wiring, and emergency circuits. In reviewing stage electrical systems, determine the condition of the control board, work lighting, stage electrical loft, balcony rail lighting, spotlight booth and orchestra pit fixtures, and auditorium ante-proscenium sidewall lighting capacity. In assessing the condition of stage rigging, inspect the gridiron, loading bridges, head block and beam, fly gallery, pipe battens, and pinrails. By necessity, this is a cursory suggestion list. A theater consultant can prove invaluable in helping you and your architect determine theater condition.

Management

Space requirements for the management and operation of a theater have increased since the days of vaudeville. Fortunately, many older theaters were constructed in a multi-use retail development, as a part of an office building, or with storefronts flanking the entry. Often, as pointed out in the Aurora, Seattle, Columbus, and Baraboo case studies, adjacent space can be utilized to consolidate administrative offices within the project property.

With box-office management for subscription programming growing somewhat complex over time—and with the increased demand for public relations, fundraising, promotion, booking, resident production, and seasonal calendars—it is likely that this part of the theater's function will require pushing a few walls out or even adding rooms or other space.

Analysis of existing office space, such as the following areas, will yield the framework from which alternatives can be developed.

Box office. Can it accommodate full-capacity, in-house ticket sales (including phone charges), computer terminals, mail orders, reserved seating, and subscription programming?

Administrative offices. How large a staff can existing administrative space accommodate? Where are the offices located in relationship to the stagehouse? Would particular areas accept nondisruptive expansion? Are there restrooms to serve administrative offices? Is there a reception area?

Stage manager's office. Does the stagehouse contain space for use by the resident stage manager?

Staff lockers and dressing rooms. Is space available or adaptable for use by ushers and stagehands?

A BRIEF PRIMER ON ADAPTIVE USE FINANCING

The financial sequence of movie palace planning involves three major areas of expenditures and investment: acquisition, alteration, and operation. In some cases, such as the

Title to the Ohio Theatre in Columbus was secured prior to fundraising for reactivation.

Tampa Theatre, Ohio Theatre, Powell Hall, and Madison Civic Center, the initial acquisition of title to the property is secured before fundraising and reconstruction. Sometimes an endowment enables a group to purchase a theater outright (St. Louis). In other cases, a municipality receives the building as a gift or purchases it with its own funds, often generated through bond issues. In still other cases, early fundraising attempts are adequately successful to meet the initial cost of outright acquisition, including short-term, high interest loans (Columbus).

Development financing pays for the production of all preliminary studies of the project, including the preparation of lender, investor, and developer feasibility packages designed to inform and/or attract each of these respective parties. If the feasibility package is effectively and thoroughly prepared, construction financing is often more readily secured. Construction funds are generally borrowed for a relatively short term at a relatively high rate of interest, and are usually repaid with monies flowing from the permanent financing. Development money can come from public subscriptions, the developer, or (with decreasing frequency) various governmental programs. Construction loans are made by commercial banks at commercial rates, and many developers have existing relationships with such lenders that can be helpful.

The greatest funding challenge lies in the acquisition of permanent financing, the centerpiece of which is usually a long-term, low interest mortgage backed by equity capital.

Generally, institutions that lend mortgage money will insist on a loan-to-value ratio of 75 percent. This means that for a project having total economic value, say, of $1 million, the maximum mortgage would equal 75 percent of that, or $750,000. In reuse projects, however, the lender might risk only 60 or 65 percent of the total project value. The debt coverage factor, which involves the relationship between net income and debt service, normally in the low end of the 20 to 40 percent range, will fall closer to the high figure in reuse projects. Thus, the net income would have to be 40 percent greater than the debt service on a given mortgage in order for the lender to agree to award the loan.

The risks involved in reuse projects (i.e., the unexpected and costly problems that can arise during development and after completion) cause the lenders to secure their money with a larger margin of safety. If the debt service on a $2-million reuse project is $160,000 per year, the lender will want a net income projection of $224,000, or a debt coverage factor of 1.4 percent. Standard sources for mortgage money include commercial banks, life insurance companies, savings banks, real estate investment trusts (REIT), savings and loan associations, pension funds, and private investors.

The percentage of a project's total costs unmet by the mortgage must be met by equity—capital money invested directly in the project by individuals and institutions desiring relatively high returns on their investment. (Nonprofit organizations may be able to secure equity and mortgage capital at

Construction underway to transform Winston-Salem's Carolina Theatre into the Roger L. Stevens Center for the Performing Arts was financed through a multitude of sources.

rates lower than those applicable to profit-making companies.)

The relationship between the mortgage interest rate, capital equity yield, projected net income, and total project value determine the economic feasibility of a project. Often, the margins of viability are extremely narrow. In projects designed for profit, a key consideration is the rate of taxation, since net income is computed after taxes and operating expenses.

The thoroughness with which the market research and subsequent public relations phases of the project are accomplished can bear fruit in municipal willingness to permit and arrange a package of tax abatements, deferments, and/or other incentives. In addition, the sponsor should work closely with state and local authorities to take advantage of the various federal programs designed to promote the development and reclamation of downtown areas.

SALESMANSHIP AND THE FEASIBILITY PACKAGE

Whether the projected reuse of a given movie palace is a private, public, or municipal venture, the chief considerations are primarily economic. The proposed conversion of a structure from presumed exhaustion to new life and expanded function must be economically feasible in order to attract the financiers requisite for project completion. The project's objectives and goals must be measured against renovation cost, anticipated revenues generated by the converted facility, and community need for such a facility and its programming. The cost of financing will help define the scope of the theater reuse project.

In many such endeavors, the salesmanship of the sponsor —both in convincing a community that it will be the better for a restored and reprogrammed movie palace, and in convincing lenders that their money will be well invested in such a project—can be as important as the features of the project itself.

Market research is helpful in determining the goods and services a community thinks would help to enrich its life. If theater revitalization costs must be assessed in relationship to the willingness of a community to subsidize, directly or indirectly, an increase in the local quality of life, the sponsor must demonstrate that the project will provide just such an increase as that community wants. The more successful the transmission of that message, the greater will be the willingness of the community to provide the necessary subsidies.

Adaptive reuse is a relatively new urban strategy with a track record insufficient for assessing its future economic performance. The sound estimation of total project costs from beginning until revenue generation on opening night is essential. Therefore, the sponsor should take care to assemble a development team of architects and contractors whose experience in adaptive reuse projects—preferably theater reuse projects—enables them to project accurate cost estimates. Although it may seem a "chicken-and-egg" dilemma that the feasibility study itself in part determines the upper limit of viable investment, the study nonetheless is more crucial in reuse projects than in new construction.

Is the project feasible?

The feasibility of a theater reuse project will depend on the combined findings of preliminary studies of the structure: its physical condition, location and context, market, and historic significance. Information gathered during feasibility studies will help to illuminate the original development objectives, and before schematic design development can proceed, the following areas of a feasibility study require exploration and analysis.

Condition and technical capacity of the theater. This section of the study should include summary descriptions of a comprehensive property analysis as discussed in "Looking Under the Dust." A structural analysis, equipment inventory, and information on state of repair and opportunities for improvements and restoration should be highlighted, as should the potential of the structure to satisfy all local city ordinances and fire codes.

Location, context, and site. What is the immediate development context of the theater (freestanding, office building, low-rise rental complex, etc.)? Is the theater accessible to the general public? What is the condition of the surrounding neighborhood? Does the city have plans or commitments to revitalize the neighborhood? What is the theater's proximity to parking and public transportation? What is the patron to parking space ratio within a one- to three-block walking distance from the theater entrance?

Market. What is the population of the area to be served? Is there demand for additional performing arts space? How many similar facilities exist and what is their proximity to the property in question? What financing opportunities exist? Is an audience survey necessary? What is the potential of theater rental as a source of income? Are there a sufficient number of community-based performing arts groups to provide income at a reduced rental rate? Is there an opportunity to promote mixed use of the theater, that is, to serve conventions, meetings, lectures, and other nonperforming arts-related events? Do demographic studies reveal information or trends that would support or discourage particular use?

Historic significance. What is the theater's role in local (or even national) history? Who was the original architect? When was the theater constructed? Are there any unusual or unique design characteristics? What is the decorative theme? Under what circumstances and to what degree has the theater been altered over time? How is the theater perceived by the community?

A National Historic Site, the Brown Grand Theatre in Concordia, Kansas, is an important local institution as well. Limestone for the building's foundation was quarried at a farm south of town, and local residents pass stories of its builder and the excitement surrounding its construction to their children and grandchildren.

Remember that the feasibility study is the black-and-white proof of a sponsor's confidence in the project. As such, it should be a carefully prepared, graphically attractive, succinct, and comprehensive document.

THE PROJECT PROPOSAL

A key component of the feasibility package is the project proposal. Because the specific economic climate of a city or region will influence the design and target audience of each reuse project, the following issues should be enunciated clearly in a project proposal.

Reuse concept.   State the history of the project, operating premise, goals, and development objectives (i.e., historic significance, home for a symphony, benefits as a performing arts resource).

Market.   Indicate the number of competing facilities in relationship to the total economic demand for the adaptive use. Clarify the advantages of adaptive use over conventional new construction.

Course of action.   Chart the development process step-by-step.

Alternative concepts for reprogramming and restoration. The heart of the proposal should be supported by and connected to the economic consequence of each concept. Drawings, architectural schemes, and other graphic material can be used to express these concepts.

Organizational structure.   Include a roster of the key players, and their responsibilities and relationships.

Enumeration of capital and operating costs.   Present funding alternatives (i.e., public, semipublic, and private resources), fundraising plans, and anticipated budget, including itemized sources of revenue in relationship to itemized expenses.

References and related supportive materials.   Any of the dozens of successful movie theater projects may be used as a precedent and reference for new undertakings. Mix and match aspects of projects as necessary.

Documentation.   Include all calculations, formulas, figures, and additional statistics that have led to the program concepts but are inappropriate for inclusion in the main body of the proposal.

Start-up costs and considerations

Start-up costs which represent the transition from project proposal to a relit movie palace marquee generally include the following:

Code compliance.   Ready use of the theater will influence the flow of income and impact of redevelopment promotion. If the theater cannot satisfy the local building code, the project

Architect's rendering of the Indiana Theatre in
Indianapolis illustrates proposed reprogramming
concepts and reuse of various building areas.

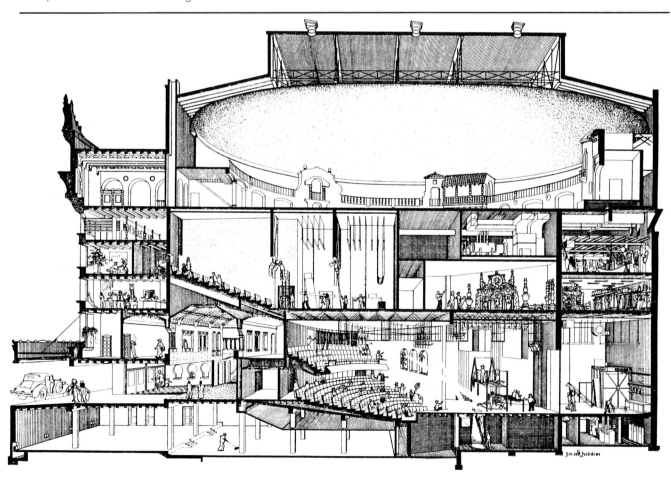

Audience comfort was a prerequisite in refurbishing Powell Hall in St. Louis. The elegance of the auditorium, pictured here, belies its excellent sight lines, acoustics, and safety features.

will suffer from both lost time and lost income. Therefore, spend your first development dollars on the following areas of the house: electrical and fire protection systems (including sprinklers and exit doors), ventilation, roof and flooring, restroom facilities, and the mechanical plant.

Audience comfort.   A comfortable audience is likely to return to the theater for quality entertainment, but an audience that cannot enjoy a performance because of annoying environmental quirks may well donate its funds and energies to another cause. Audience comfort is primarily related to general cleanliness, condition of seating, adequate ventilation, restrooms in good repair, and ease of circulation.

Performance capability.   Performers can adapt to inadequate facilities and unsatisfactory working conditions no better than an audience can adapt to intolerable seating, poor sight lines, and inconvenience. Fortunately, local rentals can often be utilized to augment broken or missing stage and sound equipment. Most large cities have theatrical equipment companies that can fully outfit a theater for sound, lighting, and other production requirements. Stageside restoration, then, can be planned incrementally if adequate stage facilities can be achieved using "make-do" arrangements.

Appearance.   Cosmetic considerations in restoration and reuse projects are important, particularly where historical accuracy is a major issue. The refurbishing of older theaters can be considered an ongoing project, however, subject to the rhythm of repair, maintenance, and upgrading. Because an

auditorium is relatively dark, touch-up work can act as a stopgap, eliminating unsightly damage. Colored light can also mask much of a theater's interior and still provide the spirit of the movie palace experience. Flexibility is the key in a theater restoration effort, for patrons, who come primarily for the performance, tend to be tolerant of, if not sympathetic to, a theater's age, as long as it does not physically interfere with their enjoyment of the activity on stage.

Publicity and promotion.   It costs very little to write and mail a news release and telephone the press to follow up on the mailing. Print and broadcast media coverage of theater restoration efforts can go a long way in promoting those efforts. Slide lectures on the history and potential of a movie palace can be presented at local civic club meetings and in turn raise public consciousness about the project and dollars for its development. (61)

MEETING THE CHALLENGE OF RENAISSANCE

Today, the frequency with which older theaters continue to reopen exceeds one book's ability to record each transformation. It is now a tested idea: the movie palace—adapted for reuse or restored for continued use as a cinema showcase

The auditorium of the beautiful Capitol Theatre in Yakima, Washington, well illustrates the potential of movie palaces great and small in cities and towns across the United States.

—is an architecturally resilient, marketable, commercially magnetic, and well-loved facility. Few restored buildings of a single type enjoy a quotient of success as high as that enjoyed by movie palaces, and few have the unique capacity of theaters to reweave vital cultural activity and economic fiber into fraying neighborhoods and downtowns.

Several key issues, extrapolated from over 50 projects completed or underway in nearly every state, characterize the diverse theater reuse scenarios.

☐ Movie palaces embody significant local and national heritage, particularly as indices of early 20th century values, design, and popular culture.

☐ Because many were originally constructed to spotlight stage shows and orchestral performances, older theaters are well suited for new use as multiple or single-purpose performing arts facilities.

☐ Although the per seat cost of each theater reuse project varies according to the requirements of its programming and the scope of its restoration, nearly all movie palaces share similar fundamental design features, constraints, and potential.

☐ A movie palace need not be restored in one herculean effort. Many of the most successful theater revitalization projects involve returning specific building areas or elements to their original grandeur as funding becomes available.

☐ Transforming an older theater into a contemporary performing arts facility is more cost-effective than building—new—its equivalent.

Movie palaces, then, offer enormous potential for a variety of community revitalization efforts. Working together toward a local renaissance, you and your fellow townspeople can explore a number of movie palace reuse options, whether cultural facility or exceptional retail mart; consider different organizational possibilities, whether nonprofit, profit-making, municipal, or a combination of these; ensure adequate financial incentives or assistance for interested sponsors; decide on a revitalization project that best answers the needs and desires of the community it will serve; approve only sensitive restoration or reuse design schemes; and, finally, support wholeheartedly the new life of the theater and its surrounding community.

RESOURCES

We offer in this section a sampling of resources—publications, audiovisual presentations, and organizations—which we hope will prove of interest and help to you as you go about relighting movie palace marquees in your own town. The catalogue is offered not as a survey of the field, but as a starting point for your own research. Most of the resources cited here lead directly to additional resources. For instance, many of the organizations produce newsletters and other publications. Many of the books include bibliographies.

While this section focuses on state and national resources, local community resources can play the strongest and most enduring role in the renaissance of a movie palace. Only those who live in a community can identify its unique resources. We attempt here to provide generic suggestions for resource development. You, in turn, can challenge your imagination to soar freely over the realm of individual possibilities so that the curtains may continue to rise.

PUBLICATIONS

Allen, Frederick Lewis. *Only Yesterday: An Informal History of the Twenties*. New York: Harper & Row, 1931.

Excellent slice-of-life narrative.

American Theatre Planning Board. *Theater Checklist: A Guide to the Planning and Construction of Proscenium and Open Stage Theaters*. Middletown, Ct.: Wesleyan University Press, 1969.

Step-by-step planning guide for developing new performing arts facilities; excellent explanation of stage design and theater terminology; ideal technical reference.

Andrews, Gregory E., ed. *Tax Incentives for Historic Preservation*. Washington, D.C.: National Trust for Historic Preservation (Preservation Press), 1981.

Essays that explain and evaluate numerous tax laws since 1966 and their affect on the financing and feasibility of historic building restoration and investment.

Armstrong, Leslie, AIA, with Roger Morgan. *Space for Dance: An Architectural Design Guide for Dance and Performing Arts Facilities*. Commissioned by the Dance and Design Arts Programs, National Endowment for the Arts, Washington, D.C. To be published: 1982.

Introduces reader to every day facility users, e.g., dancers, stage managers, facility managers. Design guidelines for arts facilities, such as theater formats, stage, public space, and space for performers. Includes case studies section of new and found spaces for the arts.

Atwell, David. *Cathedrals of the Movies: A History of British Cinemas and Their Audiences*. London: The Architectural Press, 1980.

Evaluates Britain's movie palaces constructed between 1900 and 1940 as masterpieces of imaginative design and an interesting record of popular ideas of comfort and luxury between the wars.

Bergman, Andrew. *We're In the Money! Depression America Finds Its Films*. New York: New York University Press, 1971, pp. xix-xxiii.

Useful profile of Hollywood's corporate organization on the eve of the stock market crash.

Berlingeri, Frank and H. Anthony Reilly III. *Golden Gate Theatre*. San Francisco: Golden Gate Theatre, 1980.

Monograph on the Golden Gate Theatre, restored by the Nederlander organization as a first-run Broadway road show house; excellent renovation photographs.

Brannigan-Lorelli Associates, et al. *The San Antonio Performing Arts District* (Interim Report No. 1). San Antonio: Arts Council of San Antonio, 1979.

Details the proposal to create a cultural district by centralizing the location of San Antonio's cultural and performing arts groups in two renovated downtown movie palaces; includes analysis of economic impact, management structure, and funding resources.

Chesley, Gene, ed. *The National List of Historic Theatre Buildings*. East Haddam, Ct.: League of Historic American Theatres, 1979.

Definitive listing of the national inventory of playhouses and theaters.

Coe, Linda. *Funding Sources for Cultural Facilities: Private and Federal Support for Capital Projects*. Washington, D.C.: National Endowment for the Arts (Design Arts Program), 1980.

Directory of private and federal government funding sources for cultural facilities; includes scope of projects funded.

Coe, Linda and Stephen Benedict. *Arts Management: Annotated Bibliography* (revised edition). New York: Center for Arts Information, 1980.

Comprehensive bibliography on arts management and financial issues, including useful references for marketing, public relations, planning, fundraising, organizations, volunteers, research, and policy.

Columbus Association for the Performing Arts. *The Ohio Theatre 1928-1978*. Columbus: Columbus Association for the Performing Arts, 1978.

Lavishly illustrated 50th anniversary publication documents process of saving and restoring Thomas Lamb's historic Ohio Theatre in Columbus.

Diamonstein, Barbaralee. *Buildings Reborn: New Uses, Old Places*. New York: Harper & Row, 1978.

Catalogue of more than 100 adaptive use projects, including many illustrated case studies on facilities for the arts and cultural districts.

Drexler, Arthur, ed. *The Architecture of the Ecole des Beaux Arts*. New York: The Museum of Modern Art, 1977.

Essays and excellent illustrations documenting the influential French school and its impact on Western architectural values; invaluable reference.

Dyal, Donald H. *Movie Theater Architecture: A Bibliography*. Monticello, Illinois: Vance Bibliographies, 1981.

A 15-page listing of references pertaining to the history and design of movie theater architecture.

Educational Facilities Laboratories. *The Arts in Found Places*. New York: Educational Facilities Laboratories, 1976.

Extensive review of where and how the arts have found homes in recycled buildings; more than 200 examples with special emphasis on nuts-and-bolts issues.

Educational Facilities Laboratories and Community Design Exchange. *The Arts Edge Resource Booklet*. New York: Educational Facilities Laboratories and Washington, D.C.: Community Design Exchange, 1981.

Prepared for distribution at the 1981 Arts Edge conference sponsored by the National Endowment for the Arts. Booklet includes bibliography and roster of organizations pertinent to major conference themes: arts in civic economics, artists' housing, city as stage, cultural districts, and facilities for the arts.

Gilfillen, Statler, ed. *The American Terra Cotta Index*. Palos Park, Illinois: Prairie School Press, 1972.

Index of the job files of three major midwestern terra cotta manufacturers, with numerous references to movie palace projects.

Gladson, Gene. *Indianapolis Theatres from A to Z*. Indianapolis: Gene Gladson, 1976.

Locally published survey of Indianapolis theaters, including many movie palaces.

Gomery, J. Douglas. "The Coming of Sound. Invention, Innovation, and Diffusion," Tino Balio, ed., in *The American Film Industry*. Madison: University of Wisconsin Press, 1976.

Authoritative exploration of the development and impact of sound.

Hall, Ben M. *The Best Remaining Seats*. New York: Bramhall House, 1961.

One of the first significant narratives on the history of the movie palace, with special emphasis on the life and work of Samuel "Roxy" Rothafel.

Hampton, Benjamin B. *A History of the Movies*. New York: Corvici-Friede Publishers, 1931; reprint edition, *History of the American Film Industry From Its Beginnings to 1931*. New York: Dover Publications, 1970.

An inside view of the emergence of the industry, written by one of Hollywood's first chroniclers.

Handel, Beatrice and Janet Spencer et al., eds. *The National Directory for the Performing Arts and Civic Centers*. Handel & Company, 1975.

Indispensable directory of the nation's performing arts groups and their facilities, including valuable data on cost, buildings, and capacity.

Hendon, William S., ed. *The Arts and Urban Development: Critical Comment and Discussion*. Akron: Center for Urban Studies, University of Akron: Monograph Series in Public and International Affairs, No. 12, 1980.

Theoretical analysis and examination of the influence of the arts and urban amenities on subjective business decisions.

Izenour, George C. *Theater Design*. New York: McGraw-Hill, 1978.

The definitive scholarly and architectural work on the origins, development, technology, and art of theater design, including essays on acoustical science; masterful renderings of great theaters drawn in section.

Jeffri, Joan. *The Emerging Arts: Management Survival and Growth*. New York: Praeger Publishers, 1980.

Thorough analysis of the management and representation of theater, dance, and visual arts organizations, tracing their history, development, and growth.

Jowett, Garth, for the American Film Institute. *Film: The Democratic Art*. Boston: Little, Brown and Company, 1976.

Excellent authoritative history of American film, synthesizing the economic influence of Hollywood with the social impact of moving pictures and the development of a new art form; comprehensive bibliography and appendices.

Kennedy, Joseph P., ed. *The Story of the Films*. Chicago: A. W. Shaw, 1927.

Addresses delivered at Harvard Business School by industry giants; includes speeches by Katz, Loew, and Zukor.

Kidney, Walter C. *The Architecture of Choice: Eclecticism in America 1880-1930.* New York: George Braziller, 1974.

Survey of the eclectic movement in the United States and the styles that it encompassed.

Landmarks Preservation Council of Illinois. *The North Loop Theater Study: A Performing Arts Center for Chicago.* Chicago: Landmarks Preservation Council of Illinois, 1980.

Feasibility study assessing the possibility of adaptive reprogramming for three historic movie palaces in the downtown Chicago business district; detailed architectural, marketing, and production costs.

Levin, Steven. *Paramount Theatre of the Arts.* Oakland: Paramount Theatre of the Arts, 1978.

Monograph on the history, restoration, and reopening of the Paramount in Oakland, an Art Deco masterpiece.

Lynes, Russell. *The Tastemakers: The Shaping of American Popular Taste.* New York: Dover Publications, 1980, pp. 225–234.

Analysis of the influence of movies and movie palaces on American taste and values.

Midwest Research Institute. *Economic Feasibility Study: Folly Theatre Restoration, Kansas City, Missouri.* Kansas City: Midwest Research Institute, 1978.

Economic and design feasibility study of the recently restored 1898 Folly Theatre, once a thriving burlesque, vaudeville, and comedy playhouse.

Mielziner, Jo. *Shapes of Our Theater.* Charles N. Potter, Inc., 1970.

Excellent discussion of theater design and planning by an eminent American theater consultant and set designer.

Mokwa, Michael, ed. et al. *Marketing for the Arts.* New York: Praeger Publishers, 1980.

Examines arts audiences, memberships, administrative structures, planning, and management in context of developing marketing strategies.

Mullin, Donald C. *The Development of the Playhouse: A Survey of Theater Architecture from the Renaissance to the Present.* Berkeley: University of California Press, 1970.

An excellent and scholarly treatment of evolving theater design, technology, and social context; well illustrated with useful chronologies and appendix.

Mullin, Donald C. *Origins of the Playhouse.* Cambridge: Harvard University Press, 1976.

Well-documented study of the evolution of the playhouse in the United States.

National Access Center. *504 and the Performing Arts.* Washington, D.C.: National Access Center, 1979.

Report of regulations for compliance with section 504 of the 1973 Rehabilitation Act and their affect on arts organizations.

National Endowment for the Arts. *Audience Development: An Examination of Selected Analyses and Prediction Techniques Applied to Symphony and Theater Attendance in Four Southern Cities.* New York: Publishing Center for Cultural Resources, 1981.

Discussion, with case studies, of audience analysis techniques useful to arts administrators in the development of marketing strategies.

National Endowment for the Arts/Mathtech. *Conditions and Needs of the Professional American Theater.* New York: Publishing Center for Cultural Resources, 1979.

Analysis of the state of professional theater in the United States, with recommendations for improving its financial health.

Naylor, David. *American Picture Palaces: The Architecture of Fantasy.* New York: Van Nostrand Reinhold Company, 1981.

Lavishly illustrated history of the movie palace in America. Traces theaters' development from Nickelodeon to 1930s, and chronicles their fates. Includes complete listing of the great palaces, along with their current status.

Pildas, Ave and Lucinda Smith. *Movie Palaces: Survivors of an Elegant Era.* New York: Charles N. Potter, Inc., 1980.

Color photographs of movie palace exotica, and accompanying text.

Poggi, Jack. *Theater in America: The Impact of Economic Forces.* New York: Cornell University Press, 1968, pp. 29–86.

Well-researched analysis of the economic organization of Hollywood and its impact on legitimate theater and vaudeville circuits during the emergence of popular film.

Porter, Robert, ed. *The Arts and City Planning.* New York: American Council for the Arts, 1980.

Collection of essays on urban development and the arts designed to interrelate arts agencies and city planning process; includes discussion of funding sources.

Ramsaye, Terry. *A Million and One Nights: A History of the Motion Picture.* New York: Simon & Schuster, 1926.

Contemporaneous narrative describing the early years of the industry and the art; an excellent portrait of the era with insights into the manipulations that gave America movies.

Rhode, Eric. *A History of the Cinema from Its Origins to 1970.* New York: Hill & Wang, 1976.

Analysis of the development of the motion picture, its emergence as an art form, and its international political and social reception.

Robinson, Cervin, and Rosemarie H. Bletter. *Skyscraper Style: Art Deco New York.* New York: Oxford University Press, 1976.

A detailed survey of the architectural design of high-rise structures in New York between the wars. Superb photography illuminates the informative text.

Schmertz, Mildred F., Hugh Hardy, Malcolm Holzman, and Norman Pfeiffer. "The New Madison Civic Center by Hardy Holzman Pfeiffer," *Architectural Record*. Volume 168, Number 7, July 1980, pp. 77–87.

Three-part article including a history and critique of the new facility, an itemized checklist that compares 1920s movie palace design with today's multiple-purpose performing arts requirements, and a brief, synoptic history of the building type.

Sexton, R. W. and B. F. Betts, eds. *American Theatres of To-Day, Volume I*. New York: Architectural Book Publishing Company, 1927. Sexton, R. W. *American Theatres of To-Day, Volume II*. New York: Architectural Book Publishing Company, 1930.

Contemporaneous survey of movie palace design, replete with photographs and drawings; includes valuable essays on design technology and standards.

Sharp, Dennis. *The Picture Palace*. New York: Praeger Publishers, 1969.

Survey of the development of motion picture theaters in Great Britain and the United States.

Skal, David J., ed. *Graphic Communication for the Performing Arts*. New York: Theatre Communications Group, 1981.

Well-illustrated review of graphic communications employed in the service of performing arts, particularly in managerial and marketing activities.

Sklar, Robert. *Movie Made America: A Cultural History of American Movies*. New York: Random House, 1975, pp. 1–160.

Excellent introduction to the origins and growth of the film industry; valuable social analysis of the first film titans and their first audiences.

Sklar, Robert, ed. *The Plastic Age: 1917–1930*. New York: George Braziller, 1970, pp. 1–76.

Contemporaneous essays on life during the Golden Age of Hollywood.

Tampa Bureau of City Planning. *Tampa Theatre Study*. Tampa, Florida: Tampa Bureau of City Planning, 1980.

Verifies the potential of a creative partnership between city government and a county arts agency to rescue the Tampa Theatre; includes valuable data, comparative analyses with other movie palace reuse projects, and funding alternatives.

Tidworth, Simon. *Theaters, An Illustrated History*. London: Pall Mall Press, 1973.

Generously illustrated and well-written history of theater design, from Ancient Greece to the present.

Urban Land Institute. *Adaptive Use: Development Economics, Process, and Profiles*. Washington, D.C.: Urban Land Institute, 1978.

Defines a development paradigm for adaptive use undertakings; extensive case study analysis, including sections on theaters and other cultural facilities.

Western States Arts Foundation. *The Arts Facility Planning Handbook* (working title). Santa Fe: Western States Arts Foundation, 1982.

Includes information on feasibility, real estate acquisition, design, funding (seed money and working capital), and management of facilities for the visual and performing arts. Emphasizes planning process.

Workman, Thelma. *The Best in Kansas: A History of the Brown Grand Theatre and Its Restoration*. Concordia, Kansas: Brown Grand Opera House, 1980.

Monograph on the history and restoration of a landmark vaudeville and legitimate theater.

AUDIOVISUAL PRESENTATIONS

Memoirs of a Movie Palace (1979). Produced and directed by Christian Blackwood; Commentary by Elliot Stein; Narrated by Eli Wallach. 16mm film (color), 45 minutes. Distributed by Blackwood Productions Inc., 251 West 57th Street, New York, NY 10019.

Documentary on the Loew's Kings Theater in New York includes interviews with the theater's decorator, projectionist, organist, and vaudevillian performers who played its stage. 1979 New York Emmy Award for Outstanding Documentary.

Odeon Cavalcade (1973). Produced by Greendow Productions; Directed by Barry Clayton. 16mm film (color), 35 minutes; distributed by American Federation of the Arts, 41 East 65th Street, New York, NY 10021.

Documentary exploring England's Odeon Cinema chain, the combined vision of entrepreneur Oscar Deutsch, architect Harry Weedon, and interior designer Lili Deutsch. Each of the movie palaces manifested the best of European Art Deco as a setting for the movie-going experience. Interviews with many designers and associates who helped create the chain illuminate the rise and decline of England's best known movie exhibitor.

The Paramount (1978). Produced by Stamats Communications, Inc. 11-minute multi-image dissolve production, with accompanying sound track, for two projectors. Distributed by Stamats Communications, Inc., 427 Sixth Avenue S.E., Cedar Rapids, IA 52406.

Produced to raise funds for restoration of Cedar Rapids' Paramount Theater, and primarily responsible for the funding generated for that purpose. Winner of Gold Hugo Award at Chicago Film Festival.

ORGANIZATIONS

Advisory Council on Historic Preservation, 1522 K Street, N.W., Washington, D.C. 20005. 202–254-3974

Information and advisory service to federal, state and local agencies, and to the general public; publications.

American Institute of Architects, 1735 New York Avenue, N.W., Washington, D.C. 20006. 202–626-7300

National professional organization for a diverse architectural community; 250 chapters and state organizations; extensive list of periodicals, reports, and films.

American Symphony Orchestra League, P. O. Box 669, Vienna, VA 22180. 703-281-1230

Represents interests and needs of American symphony orchestras; assists in development of new symphony orchestras; provides consultation on funding, publicity, legal concerns, and management.

American Theatre Association, 1000 Vermont Avenue, N.W., Washington, D.C. 20005. 202–628-4634

Nonprofit membership organization comprised of individuals and groups affiliated with noncommercial theater.

Business Committee for the Arts, 1501 Broadway, New York, NY 10036. 212–921-0070

National organization of business leaders working to encourage corporate support of and involvement with the arts.

Educational Facilities Laboratories/Academy for Educational Development, 680 Fifth Avenue, New York, NY 10019. 212–397-0040

Research, public service, and information disseminating organization, established to guide and encourage constructive change in education and other "people-serving" institutions.

Foundation for the Extension and Development of American Professional Theatre, 165 West 46th Street, Suite 310, New York, NY 10036. 212–869-9690

Provides consultation and guidance for professionally oriented theater and dance projects in the United States; publications include *Guidelines for Developing and Operating a Theatre* (annual), *Box Office Guidelines*, and *Subscription Guidelines*.

League of Historic American Theatres, Inc., c/o The National Theatre, 1321 E Street, N.W., Washington, D.C. 20004. 202–393-2411

Membership association including groups that own and operate theaters as performing arts facilities in historic buildings; architectural, acoustical, theater lighting, fundraising, and management consultants among roster of members; publishes newsletter, bulletins, and The National List of Historic Theatre Buildings.

National Assembly of Community Arts Agencies, 1625 I Street, N.W., Suite 725A, Washington, D.C. 20006. 202–293-6818

Membership organization of local arts centers and arts councils.

National Assembly of State Arts Agencies, 1010 Vermont Avenue, N.W., Washington, D.C. 20005. 202–347-6352

Represents the needs of state arts agencies and acts as communication link between state arts agencies, federal agencies, the U.S. Congress, the National Endowment for the Arts, and other arts service organizations.

National Endowment for the Arts, 2401 E Street, N.W., Washington, D.C. 20506. 202–634-6369

Independent federal agency funded with annual appropriations from Congress; support includes grants, information, and technical service for individuals, nonprofit tax-exempt organizations, and state and regional arts agencies; Design Arts Program administrates funds, grants, and information relating to architectural, environmental, and design research and related projects.

National Trust for Historic Preservation, 1785 Massachusetts Avenue, N.W., Washington, D.C. 20036. 202–673-4000

Chartered by U.S. Congress to facilitate public participation in preservation of buildings, sites, and objects significant in American culture and history; technical assistance, public relations, and research; publishes *Preservation News* (monthly) and *Historic Preservation Magazine* (bimonthly).

Theatre Historical Society of America, P.O. Box 101, Notre Dame, IN 46556. 219-239-5371.

Founded in 1969, THS has devoted its activities to the preservation and documentation of theaters in the United States; nonprofit membership organization; annual convention; quarterly journal; newsletter.

Theatre Communications Group, 355 Lexington Avenue, New York, NY 10017. 212–697-5320

Provides artistic, administrative, and information services to nonprofit, professional theaters and to theater artists, administrators, and technicians; fundraising and legislative information; monthly newsletter.

United States Institute for Theater Technology, 330 West 42nd Street, New York, NY 10036. 212–563-5551

Disseminates information on performing arts technology, including theater administration, design, engineering, and performing arts legislation; *USITT Newsletter* (five times a year); *Design & Technology Magazine* (quarterly).

NOTES

1. Kenneth Macgowan, *Behind the Screen: The History and Technology of the Motion Picture* (New York: Delacorte, 1965), pp. 254-55.

2. Robert Sklar, *Movie Made America: A Cultural History of American Movies* (New York: Random House, 1975), p. 16.

3. Alfred L. Bernheim, *The Business of the Theatre: An Economic History of American Theatre 1750-1932* (New York: Benjamin Bloom, 1964), p. 86.

4. Sklar, p. 46.

5. Eric Rhode, *A History of the Cinema From Its Origins to 1970* (New York: Hill & Wang, 1976), p. 43; see also Garth Jowett, for the American Film Institute, *Film: The Democratic Art* (Boston: Little, Brown and Company, 1976), pp. 30-31.

6. Robert C. Allen, "Motion Picture Exhibition in Manhattan 1906-1912: Beyond the Nickelodeon," *Cinema Journal*, vol. XXIII, no. 2 (Evanston, Illinois: spring 1979), pp. 2-15.

7. Ibid, pp. 9-10.

8. Ibid, p. 10.

9. Jowett, pp. 101-3; see also Terry Ramsaye, *A Million and One Nights: A History of the Motion Picture* (New York: Simon and Schuster, 1926), pp. 641-44.

10. Jack Poggi, *Theater in America: The Impact of Economic Forces* (New York: Cornell University Press, 1968), p. 80.

11. Samuel L. Rothafel, "What the Public Wants in a Picture Theater," *The Architectural Forum*, vol. XLII, no. 6 (New York: June 1925), p. 360 ff.

12. Douglas Gomery, "The Picture Palace: Economic Sense or Hollywood Nonsense?," *Quarterly Review of Film Studies*, vol. III, no. 1 (winter 1978), pp. 25.

13. Jowett, p. 59A.

14. Macgowan, pp. 256-7.

15. Columbus Association for the Performing Arts, *The Ohio Theatre 1928-1978* (Columbus: Columbus Association for the Performing Arts, 1978).

16. E.C.A. Bullock, "Theater Entrances and Lobbies," *The Architectural Forum*, vol. XLII, no. 6 (New York: June 1925), p. 372.

17. C. Howard Crane, "Observations on Motion Picture Theaters," *The Architectural Forum*, vol. XLII, no. 6 (New York: June 1925), p. 383.

18. Bullock, p. 372.

19. "Facts About the Uptown Theatre," *Marquee: Journal of the Theatre Historical Society*, vol. 9, no. 2 (Notre Dame, Indiana: 1977), p. 8.

20. Walter Kidney, *The Architecture of Choice: Eclecticism in America 1880-1930* (New York: George Braziller, 1974), p. 3.

21. Arthur Drexler, ed., *The Architecture of the Ecole des Beaux Arts* (New York: The Museum of Modern Art, 1977), p. 470.

22. Ibid., p. 472.

23. John Poppeliers, et. al., *What Style Is It?* (Washington, D.C.: The Preservation Press, 1977), p. 39.

24. Le Corbusier, "Guiding Principles of Town Planning," in Ulrich Conrads, ed., *Programs and Manifestoes on 20th-Century Architecture* (Cambridge: The MIT Press, 1970), p. 91.

25. Reyner Banham, *Theory and Design in the First Machine Age* (New York: Praeger Publishers, 1960), p. 215.

26. Douglas Gomery, "The Coming of Sound: Invention, Innovation, and Diffusion," in Tino Balio, ed., *The American Film Industry* (Madison: University of Wisconsin Press, 1976), pp. 193-213.

27. Ibid., p. 203.

28. Ben Schlanger, "The Small Motion Picture Theatre," *Architectural Record* (New York: June 1934).

29. David Naylor, *American Picture Palaces: The Architecture of Fantasy* (New York: Van Nostrand Reinhold Company, 1981), p. 68.

30. Andrew Bergman, *We're in the Money: Depression America and Its Films* (New York: New York University Press, 1971), pp. xx-xxii.

31. Stephen J. Sansweet, "With Ticket Sales Off, Some Movie Exhibitors Project a Bleak Future," *The Wall Street Journal*, vol. CXCVIII, no. 35 (New York: August 19, 1981), pp. 1, 19.

32. Robert E. Freeman, "Movie Palaces Have a Starring Role in Community Revitalization," *Journal of Housing* (Washington, D.C.: February 1980), p. 81.

33. Jesse Kornbluth, "The Department Store as Theater," *The New York Times Magazine* (New York: April 29, 1979), pp. 30-32 ff.

34. John Pastier, "The Architecture of Escapism," *AIA Journal*, vol. 67, no. 14 (Washington, D.C.: December 1978), pp. 26-37.

35. Sansweet, p. 1.

36. Ibid., p. 19.

37. These figures were provided by Mrs. Mary L. Bishop, Director of Building, Restoration, and Grants, Columbus Association for the Performing Arts, during a conversation in November 1981.

38. The principal source for information used in this case study is the monograph by Steve Levin, *Paramount Theatre of the Arts* (Oakland, California: Paramount Theatre of the Arts, 1978), and material provided by theater management during conversations in spring 1981.

39. Much of the data for this case study may be found in the commemorative program book issued by the Brown Grand Opera House, *The Brown Grand Theatre* (Concordia, Kansas: Brown Grand Opera House, 1980). See also Thelma Workman, *The Best in Kansas: A History of the Brown Grand Theatre and its Restoration* (Concordia, Kansas: 1980), a collection of newspaper articles published from 1973 to 1975.

40. The principal source for information used in this case study is the commemorative program book issued by the Macon Arts Council, *The Grand Opera House* (Macon, Georgia: The Macon Arts Council, 1970).

41. Tom Tomlinson, "The Grand Old Lady Starts a New Life," *Auditorium News*, vol. 15, no. 11 (November 1977), pp. 6-8.

42. Ada Louise Huxtable, "Architecture: Powell Symphony Hall," *The New York Times* (New York: January 26, 1968).

43. "A Brief History of the Community Theatre of Cedar Rapids" (Cedar Rapids, Iowa: Community Theatre of Cedar Rapids), p. 8.

44. "The Majestic Theatre: A Brief History" (Providence, Rhode Island: Trinity Square Repertory Company).

45. Charles W. Moore, *Dimensions: Space, Shape and Scale in Architecture* (New York: Architectural Record Books, 1976), p. 43.

46. Martin Filler, "In a Little Spanish Town," *Progressive Architecture*, vol. LVIII, no. 11 (Stamford, Connecticut: November 1977), p. 75.

47. Charles Moore, Gerald Allen, and Donlyn Lyndon, *The Place of Houses* (New York: Holt, Rinehart, and Winston, 1974), p. 20.

48. Henshaw Associates, Inc. and Massoni Associates, "Theatres as Resources" (Cleveland: Center for Partnerships in Resource Development, 1979), pp. 40-41.

49. Ibid., p. 40.

50. Ibid., p. 41.

51. The principal resource for information used in this case study is the monograph by Frank Berlingeri and H. Anthony Reilly III, *Golden Gate Theatre* (San Francisco: Golden Gate Theatre, 1980).

52. Robert K. Headly, "The Warner Theatre, Washington, D.C.," *Marquee: Quarterly Journal of the Theatre Historical Society*, vol. 12, nos. 1 and 2 (Notre Dame, Indiana: 1st and 2nd Quarters 1980), pp. 25-26.

53. Hardy Holzman Pfeiffer Associates, et. al., "Adapting a Movie Theater for Multi-purpose Activities," in Mildred F. Schmertz et. al., "The New Madison Civic Center by Hardy Holzman Pfeiffer Associates," *Architectural Record*, vol. 168, no. 7 (New York: July 1980) pp. 85-86.

54. Tampa Bureau of City Planning, Tampa Theatre Study (Tampa, Florida: Tampa Bureau of City Planning, 1980), p. 43.

55. Ibid., pp. 11-12.

56. Ibid., pp. 15-27.

57. Ibid., p. 9

58. Ibid., p. 74.

59. Playhouse Square Foundation, "Playhouse Square Redevelopment Project" (Cleveland: Playhouse Square Foundation, October 1979), p. 8.

60. Brannigan-Lorelli Associates, et. al., *The San Antonio Performing Arts District* (San Antonio, Texas: Arts Council of San Antonio, 1979), p. 32.

61. The concepts discussed in the first chapter of *Adaptive Use: Development, Economics, Process, and Profiles* (Washington, D.C.: Urban Land Institute, 1978) have been invaluable in the organization of the section, "Relighting the Marquee."

ILLUSTRATION CREDITS

INTRODUCTION. p. 12: Chrysalis Corp. Architects, after drawing by Newman Calloway Johnson Winfree Architects. THE PAST OF THE FUTURE. p. 14: Alan Magayne-Roshak, courtesy of University of Wisconsin-Milwaukee; pp. 16–20: Courtesy of Theatre Historical Society; pp. 22, 23: Courtesy of Theatre Historical Society; pp. 24, 25: Alan Magayne-Roshak, courtesy of University of Wisconsin-Milwaukee; p. 26: Peter Mauss; p. 27: (top) Alan Magayne-Roshak, courtesy of University of Wisconsin-Milwaukee; (bottom) Courtesy of Paramount Arts Centre; p. 28: Courtesy of Theatre Historical Society; p. 29: Chrysalis Corp. Architects; pp. 30–34: Courtesy of Theatre Historical Society; p. 35: Courtesy of Paramount Theatre; p. 36: Joseph M. Valerio; p. 37: Patrick J. Fitzgerald. REAL DREAMS. p. 38: Courtesy of Ohio Theatre; pp. 40, 41: Hardy Holzman Pfeiffer Associates; p. 42: Brannigan-Lorelli Associates, courtesy of Arts Council of San Antonio; p. 43: Courtesy of Ohio Theatre; p. 44: Hardy Holzman Pfeiffer Associates; p. 45: Dick Busher, courtesy of R. F. McCann and Company; p. 46: Chrysalis Corp. Architects; pp. 48, 49: Cathe Centorbe, courtesy of Paramount Theatre; p. 50: Wichita Eagle-Beacon, courtesy of Brown Grand Theatre; p. 51: Chrysalis Corp. Architects; p. 52: Joe DeGrandis, courtesy of Grand Opera House; p. 53: Ernie Duncan, courtesy of Capitol Theatre; pp. 55, 56: Harvey Hoshour; p. 57: Daniel Friedman; p. 58: Courtesy of Fox Theatre; p. 60: Courtesy of Powell Symphony Hall; p. 61: Chrysalis Corp. Architects; pp. 62, 63: Courtesy of Powell Symphony Hall; p. 61: Chrysalis Corp. Architects; pp. 62, 63: Courtesy of Trinity Square Repertory Company; pp. 65, 66: Wayne McCall, courtesy of Arlington Center for the Performing Arts; p. 68: (left) Courtesy of Al Ringling Theatre; (right) Courtesy of Theatre Historical Society; p. 69: Courtesy of Theatre Historical Society; p. 70: Courtesy of Golden Gate Theatre; p. 71: Daniel Friedman; p. 72: Courtesy of Theatre Historical Society; p. 73: (left) Courtesy of Theatre Historical Society; (right) Alan Magayne-Roshak, courtesy of University of Wisconsin-Milwaukee; p. 74: Hardy Holzman Pfeiffer Associates; p. 75: Norman McGrath, courtesy of Hardy Holzman Pfeiffer Associates; p. 76: Chrysalis Corp. Architects; p. 77: Courtesy of Paramount Arts Centre; p. 78: Bill Engdahl, courtesy of Paramount Arts Center; p. 80: Chrysalis Corp. Architects, after drawing by the office of John Eberson; p. 81: Courtesy of Tampa Theatre; p. 83: Chrysalis Corp. Architects; p. 85: David M. Lambert, courtesy of Newman Calloway Johnson Winfree Architects; (right) courtesy of Newman Calloway Johnson Winfree Architects; pp. 86, 87: Courtesy of Newman Calloway Johnson Winfree Architects; p. 88: Charlie Buchanan, courtesy of Newman Calloway Johnson Winfree Architects; p. 90: Brandt, courtesy of Indiana Repertory Theatre; p. 91: Peter Mauss; p. 93: Courtesy of Heinz Hall for the Performing Arts; p. 94: Brannigan-Lorelli Associates, courtesy of Arts Council of San Antonio; p. 95: Tom Sherman, courtesy of Grand Opera House. RELIGHTING THE MARQUEE. p. 96: T. Mike Fletcher, courtesy of Powell Symphony Hall; p. 98: Courtesy of Heinz Hall for the Performing Arts; p. 99: Courtesy of Theatre Historical Society; p. 100: Grieves-Armstrong-Childs Architects, courtesy of Grand Opera House; p. 101: Alan Magayne-Roshak, courtesy of University of Wisconsin-Milwaukee; p. 102: Pfuetze-Bergman Studio, courtesy of Brown Grand Theatre; pp. 103, 104: Courtesy of Theatre Historical Society; p. 106: Courtesy of Ohio Theatre; p. 107: Newman Calloway Johnson Winfree Architects; p. 109: Pfuetze-Bergman Studio, courtesy of Brown Grand Theatre; p. 110: J. W. McQuiston, courtesy of Indiana Repertory Theatre; p. 111: Courtesy of Powell Symphony Hall; p. 112: Ernie Duncan, courtesy of Capitol Theatre.